J. SHERWOOD

A Mariner's Guide
to the
Rules of the Road

William H. Tate

Naval Institute Press
Annapolis, Maryland

Preface

A Mariner's Guide to the Rules of the Road is designed to give a concise, comprehensive treatment of the rules of the road for U.S. inland waters as well as for international waters. Because the Inland Rules have not been significantly updated for many years, a good deal of court interpretation has been included. The 1972 International Rules, in the path of revisions in 1948 and 1960, are much more complete, comprehensive, and, most important, useful to the mariner. It is the opinion of the author that court interpretations of the 1972 International Rules will not significantly change the knowledge required of the mariner for several years to come.

The contents of this text were originally discussed at a Navigation Symposium held in Newport, Rhode Island, in April of 1973. The author is especially grateful to Commander F. E. Bassett, USN, Chairman of the Navigation Department at the U.S. Naval Academy, under whose guidance this text was prepared, and to the following officers who continually made their contributions and suggestions during the preparation of the text: Lieutenant Commander J. L. Roberts, USN, Lieutenant Commander A. J. Tuttle, USN, and Lieutenant Commander R. A. Smith, RN. Special thanks are also due to other members of the marine community who have made suggestions and contributions: Captain J. C. Martin, USN (Ret.), Defense Mapping Agency; Captain C. J. McGuire, USCG, U.S. Coast Guard Headquarters; Captain R. H. Terry and Commander E. J. Geissler, USCG (Ret.), Maine Maritime Academy; Captain E. D. Cassidy, USCG, U.S. Coast Guard Academy; Professor Lester A. Dutcher, State University of New York Maritime College; and Commander O. E. Thompson, USMS, U.S. Merchant Marine Academy.

William H. Tate
Lieutenant, U.S. Naval Reserve
Assistant Professor of Nautical Science
Florida Institute of Technology
Jensen Beach, Florida

Any opinions or assertions contained in this text are those of the author and do not necessarily reflect the views of the Navy or the naval service as a whole.

Contents

Introduction
to the
Rules of the Road

The navigation of a vessel on the high seas is subject to the International Regulations for Preventing Collisions at Sea (commonly called the International Rules of the Road). The International Regulations for Preventing Collisions at Sea, 1972, became effective on 15 July 1977. This effective date follows by one year the date on which a sufficient number of nations approved the new rules. The 1972 rules are the outgrowth of an International Conference held in London during October 1972. Fifty-two governments participated in the conference, which was held under the auspices of the Intergovernmental Maritime Consultative Organization (IMCO). Previous revisions were made by similar conferences held in 1948 and 1960. The International Rules are being given force by separate statutes in each of the participating maritime nations.

Rule 1 of the International Regulations for Preventing Collisions at Sea, 1972, begins as follows:

These rules shall apply to all vessels upon the high seas and in all waters connected therewith navigable by seagoing vessels.

Nothing in these rules shall interfere with the operation of special rules made by an appropriate authority for roadsteads, harbours, rivers, lakes or inland waterways connected with the high seas and navigable by seagoing vessels. Such special rules shall conform as closely as possible to these rules.

The United States has special rules for the waters of the United States and her territories, which are authorized by Rule 1. The special rules of primary importance are the Inland Rules of the Road, which are supplemented by the Pilot Rules for Inland Waters. These rules do not apply to the Great Lakes or Western Rivers, each area being governed by a separate set of rules.

The purpose of the rules of the road is to prevent collisions. Captain Raymond F. Farwell noted that "nearly all marine collisions follow violations of the rules of the road. The inference is

Fig. 1 *Boundary* line for inland waters, as shown on a chart.

Relevant excerpt from Colregs Demarcation Lines: "A line drawn from Cape Charles Light to Cape Henry Ligpt."

that the rules, if implicitly obeyed, are practically collision-proof."

Officers at sea must have such a thorough understanding of the rules that they can recognize each situation and know the actions required of their vessel without hesitation. This is no small task, particularly when faced with the complexity of the special rules for the inland waters of the United States.

The following general principles emphasize the importance of the rules and assist in placing the rules in the proper perspective:

Rules apply according to location of vessel

Rules of the road are mandatory

Obedience must be timely

Rules apply alike to all vessels.

RULES APPLY ACCORDING TO LOCATION OF VESSEL

Unfortunately for the mariner, there is no one set of rules to be followed at all times and in all locations. The purpose of the rules is to prevent collisions, yet the confusion caused by having boundary lines which separate one set of rules from another may in itself contribute to some collisions.

The rules which are the subject of this text are published in the Coast Guard pamphlet *Rules of the Road, International—Inland* (CG-169). Changes are published in the weekly Notice to Mariners, as requested by the U.S. Coast Guard.

When planning a voyage to a foreign country, a mariner should consult the *Sailing Directions* in order to become familiar with the special rules (if any) for the waters to be traversed. There will also be differences found in the buoyage systems of other countries.

Because of the significant differences between the International Rules and the Inland Rules, it is extremely important that the mariner be familiar with the rules which apply to the geographic location of his vessel, and be aware of the boundary whenever he approaches it. The lines are normally shown on navigational charts, and are described for many locations in CG-169 (Figure 1). Section 82.2 of the Code of Federal Regulations provides general rules (illustrated in Figure 2) for the locations not mentioned:

> At all buoyed entrances from seaward to bays, sounds, rivers, or other estuaries for which specific lines are not described in this part, the waters inshore of a line approximately parallel with the general trend of the shore, drawn through the outermost buoy or other aid to navigation of any system of aids, are inland waters, and upon them the Inland Rules and Pilot Rules made in pursuance thereof apply.

RULES OF THE ROAD ARE MANDATORY

Both the International and the Inland Rules are statutory—they are laws which can be found in Title 33 of the United States Code. The Inland Rules provide for a penalty for vessels navigated in violation of the rules and regulations. The International Rules contain no such penalty, as enforcement is not generally feasible. The rules are applied by courts of law to determine how damages will be divided by vessels involved in collisions.

The Pilot Rules are not statutory, but are regulations found in Title 33 of the Code of Federal Regulations. The authority for the Coast Guard to establish the regulations is given in the Inland Rules. Many students of the rules question

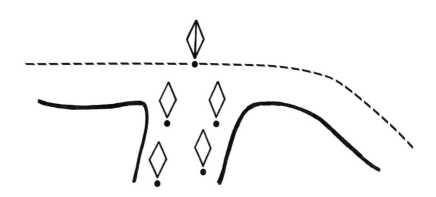

Fig. 2 General rules for lines setting off inland waters.

the existence of the Pilot Rules in addition to the Inland Rules, so some clarification may be of benefit. Whenever a law is passed by Congress, there will be at least one institution responsible for enforcing the law. Often the law itself contains only the most important provisions, and the appropriate institution must provide the missing details when it issues its regulations. The first step an institution must take is to interpret the law in question in order to accomplish the purpose of the law within certain inherent constraints. Such is the case with the Coast Guard, which is responsible for the regulations that implement as well as supplement the Inland Rules. The role of the Coast Guard is described in the following excerpt from the Inland Rules:

> The Secretary of the Department in which the Coast Guard is operating shall establish such rules to be observed . . . by steam vessels in passing each other and as to the lights and day signals to be carried . . . by ferryboats, by vessels and craft of all types when in tow of steam vessels or

operating by hand power or horsepower or drifting with the current, and by any other vessels not otherwise provided for, not inconsistent with this Act, as he from time to time may deem necessary for safety, which rules are declared special rules duly made by local authority.

The lack of provisions for lights and shapes for many categories of vessels shows an obvious need for supplementation of the Inland Rules.

The legal status of the Pilot Rules can best be summarized in the words of a court of appeals:

> Pilot Rules have been promulgated for each set of statutory navigation rules. Because they have been promulgated pursuant to authority delegated in the statutory rules, the Pilot Rules have the same force and effect as the statutory rules.[1]

Thus the mariner is governed by the statutory International and Inland rules, and the Pilot Rules which have the force of law. There are only two grounds on which departure from the rules will be excused by the courts. The first is given by Rule 2(b) of the International Rules (the General Prudential Rule for inland waters is very similar):

> In construing and complying with these rules due regard shall be had to all dangers of navigation and collision and to any special circumstances, including the limitations of the vessels involved, which may make a departure from these rules necessary to avoid immediate danger.

Secondly, a departure from the rules which was not required by special circumstances will be excused only if the offending vessel can show that such departure could not have contributed to the collision. As expressed by a court of appeals:

When fault consists in breach of statutory rule intended to prevent collisions, burden rests upon ship of not showing merely that her fault might not have been one of causes, or that it probably was not, but that it could not have been.[2]

OBEDIENCE MUST BE TIMELY

The International Rules make this requirement very definite:

Rule 8—Action to Avoid Collision
    (a) Any action taken to avoid collision shall, if the circumstances of the case admit, be positive, made in ample time and with due regard to the observance of good seamanship.
    (b) Any alteration of course and/or speed to avoid collision shall, if the circumstances of the case admit, be large enough to be readily apparent to another vessel observing visually or by radar; a succession of small alterations of course and/or speed should be avoided.
    (c) If there is sufficient sea room, alteration of course alone may be the most effective action to avoid a close-quarters situation provided that it is made in good time, is substantial and does not result in another close-quarters situation.
    (d) Action taken to avoid collision with another vessel shall be such as to result in passing at a safe distance. The effectiveness of the action shall be carefully checked until the other vessel is finally past and clear.

1. *First National Bank of Chicago* v. *Material Service Corporation*, C.C.A. 1976, 544 F. 2d 911.

2. *Diesel Tanker F.A. Verdon, Inc.* v. *Stakeboat No. 2*, C.A.N.Y. 1965, 340 F. 2d 465.

(e) If necessary to avoid collision or allow more time to assess the situation, a vessel shall slacken her speed or take all way off by stopping or reversing her means of propulsion.

The Inland Rules contain no such discussion, but the words of a district court demonstrate that the intention is the same:

Precautions required by law to be taken when there is a risk of collision must be taken in time to be effective against such risk, or they will constitute no defense if collision occurs.[3]

RULES APPLY ALIKE TO ALL VESSELS

All vessels, public and private, regardless of size, speed, or nationality, must obey the rules.

3. The *Westhall*, D.C. Va. 1899, 153 F. 1010.

PART I
Inland Waters

1 Introduction to the Rules for Inland Waters

The purpose of this chapter is to familiarize the reader with certain principles of marine collision law as exercised in the courts of the United States. In addition, certain terms that are basic to the understanding of the rules themselves will be defined.

RULES MODIFIED BY COURT INTERPRETATION

Article 29, the "Rule of Good Seamanship" (Chapter 7), states that special circumstances may require precautions in addition to the literal requirements of the rules. Over the years numerous court decisions have construed various rules together with Article 29. CG-169 does not discuss the additional requirements which have evolved from the court decisions. It is because of the necessity to understand the rules in light of court interpretation that texts such as this one exist. The courts have also provided legal meanings for certain phrases used in the rules, such as "moderate speed," "proper lookout," and "risk of collision."

The Inland Rules state that the Pilot Rules will not be "inconsistent with the provisions of this act." The outcome of a collision case may be determined by the court ruling that a Pilot Rule is inconsistent with the Inland Rules, and therefore invalid. The courts have also given meaning to ambiguous phrases in the Pilot Rules.[1] Other provisions have been found applicable only to a specific approach situation, while the wording of the rule may imply that it applies to all situations.[2] The Coast Guard could eliminate a good deal of confusion by revising certain portions of the Pilot Rules.

1. The requirement for signals when "passing or meeting at a distance within half a mile of each other" has been interpreted by the courts to mean signals are required when the closest point of approach (CPA) will be within half a mile — not when the vessels are actually at a range of one-half mile from each other. *See* page 39.
2. An example is paragraph 80.3(a) of the Pilot Rules. For a discussion, *see* page 39 of this text.

JURISDICTION IN COLLISION CASES

Federal courts, sitting as courts of admiralty, have jurisdiction over cases of collision between vessels on public navigable waters (defined as waters used, or capable of being used, in interstate commerce). Collision cases begin in a federal district court, and can be appealed to a circuit court of appeals, and in some cases, to the United States Supreme Court.

State courts have jurisdiction when collisions occur on a lake wholly within a state, and concurrent jurisdiction when collisions occur in any portion of public navigable waters within a state. Most of the latter cases are tried in federal courts.

LEGAL PERSONALITY OF A VESSEL

In courts of the United States a vessel is assumed to be the wrongdoer when collision follows a violation of the rules of the road. When a vessel is libeled, she is sued "in rem." The vessel is taken into custody until the claims against her are satisfied, unless the owners obtain her release by paying an amount equal to her appraised valuation, or post a bond double the amount of existing liens. A vessel may be sold to satisfy the judgment against her. The sale gives the vessel a new lease on life, as the owners are free of any old claims against her.

LIMITED LIABILITY OF A VESSEL

The principle of limited liability serves to protect the owner against the possibility of losing all of his resources because of a negligent master. The limit of liability is the value of the vessel at the expiration of the voyage, plus "pending freight." It is possible then that a vessel totally at fault, but also totally lost and with no pending freight, could leave the injured vessel unable to recover anything for damage either to herself or her cargo. The liability for death or personal injury is a maximum of $60 per gross register ton where the remaining value of the ship is less than that amount.

If the circumstances of a collision are found not to be beyond the control of the owners, and their fault can be shown, limitation of liability can be denied. In such a case, levies can be placed against the owners' entire fleet, if necessary, to satisfy a judgment.

Naval vessels and other public vessels are not subject to lien, and cannot be taken into custody. The United States is sued as an owner "in personam," rather than the vessel being sued "in rem."

COMPARATIVE NEGLIGENCE

For many years the courts of the United States required two vessels involved in a collision to share the total damages equally if both were guilty of a rule violation that contributed to the collision. In 1975 the Supreme Court adopted what might be called a rule of comparative negligence:

> We hold that when two or more parties have contributed by their fault to cause property damage in a maritime collision or stranding, liability for such damage is to be allocated among the parties proportionately to the comparative degree of their fault, and that liability for such damages is to be allocated equally only when the parties are equally at fault or when it is not possible fairly to measure the comparative degree of their fault.

If one vessel is solely at fault, she is liable for the

total damage to the other, subject only to the provisions of the Limited Liability Acts.[3]

INEVITABLE COLLISION

If neither vessel is found at fault in a collision, each must bear its own loss. Such cases are rare; the following rulings illustrate the thinking of the courts:

> Finding that collision between vessels was result of inevitable accident is not to be lightly arrived at, and the burden of proof is heavily upon party asserting that defense to affirmatively establish that accident could not have been prevented by use of that degree of reasonable care and attention which the situation demanded, and that there was no intervening act of negligence on its part.[4]

> Where a collision between steamships occurs, exclusive of natural causes and without the fault of either party, the loss must rest where it falls, but such a case requires that both parties must have endeavored by every means in their power, with due care and caution and a proper display of nautical skill, to prevent the collision.[5]

> To exonerate a steamer from liability . . . on the ground of inevitable accident arising from a latent defect in her machinery, it must be shown that such defect could not have been discovered by a person of competent skill in the exercise of ordinary care, and further, that such defect necessarily caused the accident.[6]

3. *U.S.* v. *Reliable Transfer Company, Inc.*, 1975, 44L. Ed. 251.
4. *Swenson* v. *The Argonaut*, C.A.N.J. 1953, 204 F. 2d 636.
5. The *Djerissa*, D.C. Va. 1919, 2558 F. 949, affirmed 267 F. 115.
6. The *Homer*, D.C. Wash. 1900, 99 F. 795.

DEFINITIONS

The following definitions will aid in the discussion of the Inland Rules and the Pilot Rules for Inland Waters.

Sailing vessel Every steam vessel which is under sail and not under steam is to be considered a sailing vessel, and every vessel under steam, whether under sail or not, is to be considered a steam vessel. (Article 1)

Steam vessel Any vessel propelled by machinery. (Article 1)

Underway Not at anchor, or made fast to the shore, or aground. (Article 1)

Visible When applied to lights, shall mean visible on a dark night with a clear atmosphere. (Article 1)

Fishing Fishing with nets, lines, or trawls. (Article 26)

Short blast A blast of the whistle of about one second's duration. (Pilot Rules, Subparagraph 80.03(a)(1))

Prolonged blast A blast of from four to six seconds' duration, used only as a fog signal in inland waters. (Article 15)

Long blast While not defined in the rules, a blast of eight to ten seconds' duration would not be confused with the other signals.

Blast of unspecified duration Article 15(c) prescribes fog signals for a sailing vessel underway, without specifying their duration—it is difficult to control the duration of a blast on many mechanical fog horns. The sound of these signals will be distinctive as they are given on the fog horn, while steam vessels give fog signals on a whistle or siren.

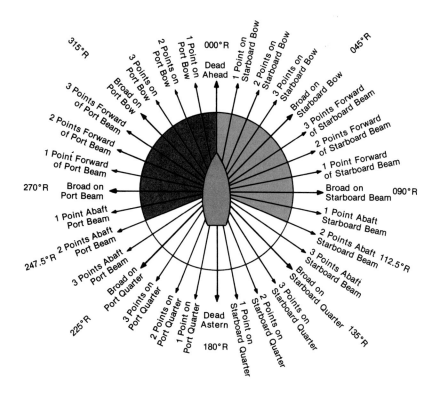

Relative bearings Figure 3 is provided to aid in familiarizing the reader with the use of "points" in expressing relative bearings. A point equals 11-1/4 degrees, 32 points equals 360 degrees, etc.

Fig. 3 Relative bearing using points.

2 Lights and Shapes

The basic purpose of lights is to warn vessels of the presence or approach of other vessels. Lights aid in determining the course and aspect of vessels underway. In some cases, lights indicate a vessel which is restricted in her ability to maneuver, either because of physical characteristics or because of the activity in which she is engaged. The prescribed shapes serve the same purpose during the day.

Article 1 of the Inland Rules states:

> The rules concerning lights shall be complied with in all weathers from sunset to sunrise, and during such time no other lights which may be mistaken for the prescribed lights shall be exhibited.

No mention is made of the use of lights during the day, but common sense and good seamanship would dictate that lights be displayed any time a vessel is being navigated in conditions of restricted visibility.

Keep in mind that all vessels must display some sort of navigation lights when underway at night. For a small boat, this may mean only a single white light visible from all directions. For larger vessels, which carry more than one light, there must always be at least one light visible from every direction.

The Inland Rules make no distinction between a vessel underway with way on and a vessel underway with no way on. Vessels display the same lights at all times while underway, even if dead in the water.

TERMS

The following terms will be used in this text to describe the lights and shapes displayed in the inland waters of the United States.

Masthead light A 20-point white light at the forward masthead, showing an arc of light from dead ahead to 2 points abaft the beam on both sides.

Range light A white light abaft of and higher than the masthead light. It is in line with the masthead light (forms a range) if the vessel is seen from dead ahead. It is a 32-point light, except for seagoing steam vessels which may show a 20-point light.

Sternlight A 12-point white light showing 6 points from right aft on each side. In inland waters, it is required only when there is no other light visible from aft.

Fig. 4 Double frustum of a cone.

Sidelights A red light on the port side, and a green light on the starboard side. Both are 10-point lights showing from dead ahead to 2 points abaft the beam on their respective sides.

Towing masthead lights and towing range lights Two or more lights of the same character as the 20-point masthead light or the 32-point range light.

Amber pushing lights Two amber lights displayed in a vertical line at the stern, showing over the same arc as would a 12-point sternlight.

Double frustum of a cone A shape formed by placing two frustums base to base.

The lights that vessels are required to show in the inland waters of the United States are illustrated below.

Fig. 5 Seagoing Steam Vessel (operating both on the high seas and on inland waters). Inland Rules, Articles 2, 10.

STEAM VESSELS UNDERWAY

Figure 5

Required lights

Masthead light (20-point)
Sidelights (10-point)
Sternlight (12-point)

Other lights

For a seagoing steam vessel of any length, a 20-point, after-range light is optional in the Inland Rules.

Notes

This provision allows a vessel (other than an air-cushion vessel) in inland waters to show the same lights that she would show when subject to the International Rules.

Steam Vessels Underway (cont.)

The Motorboat Act of 1940 permits vessels of less than 65 feet in length to exhibit the lights required by the International Rules.

Figure 6

Required lights

Masthead light (20-point)
Range light   (32-point)
Sidelights   (10-point)

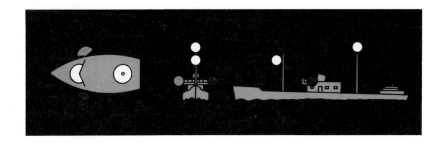

Fig. 6 Steam Vessel (except seagoing vessels and ferryboats). Inland Rules, Articles 2, 10.

STEAM VESSELS TOWING ASTERN

Figure 7

Required lights

3 towing masthead lights (20-point)
Sidelights   (10-point)
12-point sternlight required if optional range light not shown

Other lights

32-point range light is optional (not shown in Figure 7)

In lieu of the sternlight, a small white light may be used for the tow to steer by, but it shall not be visible forward of the beam.

Notes

Length of tow is not a factor in determining the lights to be shown.

Hawser lengths are limited by law to 450 feet.

Fig. 7 Towing astern — towing masthead lights. Inland Rules, Article 3.

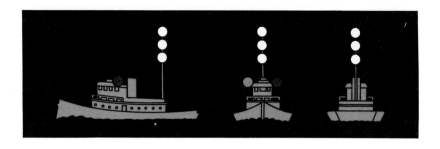

Fig. 8 Towing astern — towing range lights. Inland Rules, Article 3.

Fig. 9 Towing alongside — towing masthead lights. Inland Rules, Article 3.

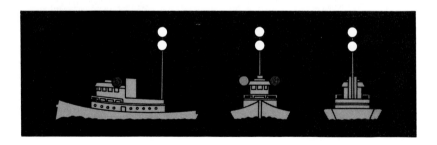

Fig. 10 Towing alongside — towing range lights. Inland Rules, Article 3.

Steam Vessels Towing Astern (cont.)

<u>Figure 8</u>

Required lights

3 towing range lights (32-point)
Sidelights (10-point)

STEAM VESSELS TOWING ALONGSIDE

<u>Figure 9</u>

Required lights

2 towing masthead lights (20-point)
Sidelights (10-point)
12-point sternlight required if optional range light is not shown

Other lights

32-point range light is optional (not shown in Figure 9)

<u>Figure 10</u>

Required lights

2 towing range lights (32-point)
Sidelights (10-point)

STEAM VESSELS PUSHING TOW AHEAD

Figure 11

Required lights

2 towing masthead lights	(20-point)
Sidelights	(10-point)
2 amber pushing lights at the stern	(12-point)

Other lights

32-point range light is optional (not shown in Figure 11)

Note

The two amber pushing lights are shown only when pushing ahead *and* displaying the 20-point towing masthead lights.

Figure 12

Required lights

2 towing range lights	(32-point)
Sidelights	(10-point)

SAILBOATS AND VESSELS BEING TOWED

Figure 13

Required lights

Sidelights (10-point)
Sternlight (12-point)

Fig. 11 Pushing ahead — towing masthead lights. Inland Rules, Article 3.

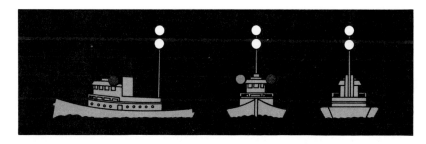

Fig. 12 Pushing ahead — towing range lights. Inland Rules, Article 3.

Fig. 13 Sailboats and vessels being towed (vessels in tow except barges, canal boats, scows, and other vessels of nondescript type). Inland Rules, Article 5. *See* Pilot Rules for the latter types.

Fig. 14 Vessel engaged in fishing. Inland Rules, Article 9, and Pilot Rules, Section 80.32a.

Fig. 15 Steam pilot vessel on station — not at anchor. Inland Rules, Article 8.

Fig. 16 Steam pilot vessel on station — at anchor. Inland Rules, Article 8.

VESSELS ENGAGED IN FISHING

Figure 14

Required lights

Where best seen—red over white (32-point)

Dayshape

Basket. All vessels or boats fishing with nets or lines or trawls, when underway, shall in daytime indicate their occupation by displaying a basket where it can best be seen. When at anchor, the basket will be placed to show the direction toward the nets or gear.

STEAM PILOT VESSELS ON STATION

Figure 15

Required lights

At masthead—white over red (32-point)
Sidelights   (10-point)
Flare-up light, maximum interval 15 minutes

Note

Sailing pilot vessels do not show the red light at the masthead, and show sidelights only on the approach of other vessels.

Figure 16

Required lights

At masthead—white over red (32-point)
Flare-up light, maximum interval 15 minutes

VESSELS AT ANCHOR AND AGROUND
(Court Interpretation)

Figure 17

Required lights

One 32-point white light forward

Dayshape

Black ball in forward part of vessel, required if length of vessel greater than 65 feet

Note

In special anchorage area: a vessel not more than 65 feet in length is not required to show anchor lights; where two or more barges, canal boats, scows, or other nondescript craft are tied together as a unit, the anchor light need be displayed only on the vessel that has its anchor down.

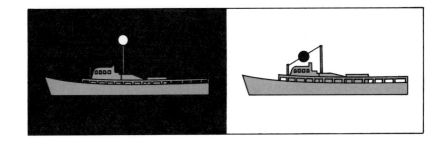

Fig. 17 Vessel less than 150 feet in length — at anchor or aground. Inland Rules, Article 11, and Pilot Rules, Section 80.25.

Figure 18

Required lights

One 32-point white light forward
One 32-point white light aft and at least 15 feet lower than forward light

Dayshape

Black ball in forward part of vessel

Note

In special anchorage area: a barge, canal boat, scow, or other nondescript craft may show only one white light, and if two or more are tied together and anchored as a unit, only the vessel with anchor down must display a light.

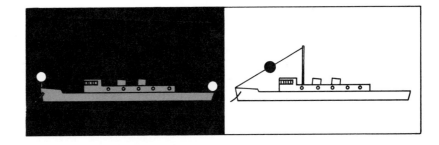

Fig. 18 Vessel 150 feet and upward in length — at anchor or aground. Inland Rules, Article 11, and Pilot Rules, Section 80.25.

Fig. 19 Towing a submerged object — towing masthead lights. Pilot Rules, Sections 80.18, 80.24.

Fig. 20 Towing a submerged object — towing range lights. Pilot Rules, Sections 80.18, 80.24.

VESSELS TOWING SUBMERGED, OR PARTLY SUBMERGED, OBJECTS (when no signals can be displayed on the object being towed)

Figure 19

Required lights

4 towing masthead lights, white-red-red-white (20-point)

Sidelights (10-point)

12-point sternlight required if optional range light not shown

Other lights

32-point range light is optional (not shown in Figure 19)

Dayshapes

2 double frustums of cones, black and white horizontally striped over red, where best seen

Note

The above should be shown by a vessel minesweeping in inland waters.

Figure 20

Required lights

4 towing range lights, white-red-red-white (32-point)

Sidelights (10-point)

Dayshapes

2 double frustums of cones, black and white horizontally striped over red, where best seen

DREDGES

Figure 21

Required lights

Where best seen—2 red 32-point lights

Dredges (cont.)

White light at each corner

For scows alongside, a white light on each outboard corner

Dayshapes

Where best seen—2 red balls

Notes

A dredge working in a channel must have its anchors marked by buoys. At night the buoys must either have red lights on them or light from the plant must be thrown on them when other vessels are passing.

Pipelines attached to dredges must be lighted by a single row of amber lights, and the discharge end or both sides of an opening in a channel must be lighted by 2 red lights in a vertical line (Pilot Rules, Section 80.23).

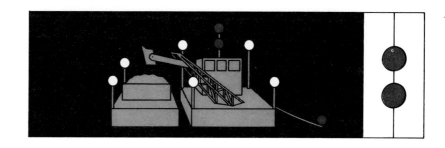

Fig. 21 Stationary dredge. Pilot Rules, Sections 80.20, 80.29.

Figure 22

Required lights

3 masthead lights, white-red-red	(20-point)
Sidelights	(10-point)
2 red lights in a vertical line at the stern	
	(12-point)
Range light	(32-point)

Dayshapes

Where best seen—2 black balls

Note

See Pilot Rules, Section 80.21(c), for lights of non-self-propelled dredge which is underway and engaged in dredging operations while being pushed ahead.

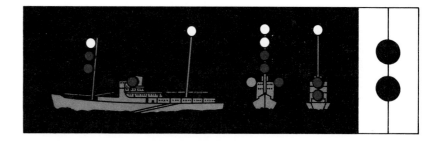

Fig. 22 Self-propelled dredge underway and engaged in dredging operations. Pilot Rules, Sections 80.21, 80.24.

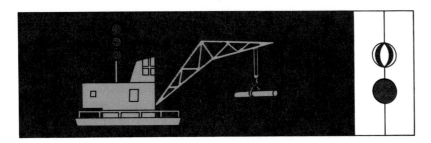

Fig. 23 Vessels moored or anchored and engaged in laying cables or pipe, submarine construction, excavation, mat sinking, bank grading, revetment, or other bank-protection operations. Pilot Rules, Section 80.22.

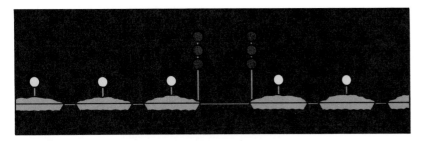

Fig. 24 Stringout of barges crossing a channel. Pilot Rules, Section 80.22(c).

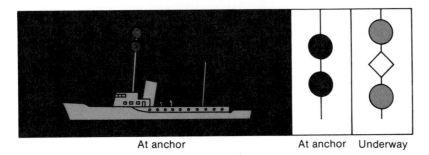

At anchor   At anchor   Underway

Fig. 25 Vessel employed in hydrographic surveying. Pilot Rules, Section 80.33.

SUBMARINE AND OTHER CONSTRUCTION

Figures 23 and 24

Required lights

Where best seen—3 red lights   (32-point)

Dayshapes

Where best seen—2 balls, black and white vertically striped over red

Notes

Anchors must be marked by buoys if working in a channel. At night the buoys must either have red lights on them or light from the plant must be thrown on them when other vessels are passing (Pilot Rules, Section 80.29).

Where a stringout of moored vessels or barges engaged in the operations crosses a channel, the stringout shall be marked by a horizontal row of amber lights, and each side of the opening by 3 red lights.

VESSELS EMPLOYED IN HYDROGRAPHIC SURVEYING

Figure 25

Notes

No special lights when underway.

When anchored in a fairway, must have flare-up light to be shown as necessary in order to attract attention.

COAST GUARD VESSELS HANDLING
OR SERVICING AIDS TO NAVIGATION

Figure 26

Notes

The display of special lights and shapes shown is optional.

Vessels, with or without tows, passing Coast Guard vessels displaying this signal, shall reduce speed sufficiently to insure the safety of both vessels, and when passing within 200 feet, their speed shall not exceed 5 miles per hour.

Dayshapes

Two balls in a vertical line, both orange and white vertically striped

Fig. 26 Coast Guard vessel handling or servicing aids to navigation. Pilot Rules, Paragraph 80.33(a).

VESSELS ALONGSIDE OR OVER A WRECK

Figure 27

Required lights

Where best seen—2 red lights   (32-point)

White light at bow and white light at stern   (32-point)

Dayshapes

Where best seen—2 double frustums of cones, both red

Fig. 27 Steam vessels, derrick boats, lighters, or other types of vessels made fast alongside a wreck, or moored over a wreck which is on the bottom or partly submerged, or which may be drifting. Pilot Rules, Sections 80.19, 80.29.

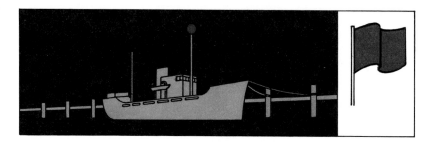

Fig. 28 Warning signal displayed while transferring dangerous cargoes. Pilot Rules, Section 80.38.

VESSELS TRANSFERRING DANGEROUS CARGOES

Figure 28

Notes

The red light is shown only while fast to a dock or berth—no special warning signal is displayed at night while at anchor.

The red flag is shown while fast to a dock or berth, or at anchor.

The red flag will be universally understood, since it is an international signal. (*See* International Code of Signals, published in the United States as H.O. 102).

SUMMARY OF IMPORTANT PROVISIONS

The lights and shapes prescribed by the International Rules are not legal in the inland waters of the United States unless specifically provided for in the Inland Rules or Pilot Rules. Flag-hoist signals from the International Code of Signals (published in the United States as H.O. 102) may be used on the high seas or in inland waters, even where not required by the rules.

The *steam vessel* in the Inland Rules and the power-driven vessel in the International Rules are both defined as "any vessel propelled by machinery." The Inland Rules have provisions which allow a power-driven vessel (other than an air-cushion vessel) to show the lights from the International Rules in inland waters. The Motorboat Act of 1940 is an amendment to the Inland Rules which changes the lighting requirements for certain steam vessels not more than 65 feet in length.

Steam vessels engaged in towing or pushing in inland waters may show the white lights either forward or aft. If shown forward, they will all be of the same character as the 20-point masthead light —"towing masthead lights." If shown aft, they will all be of the same character as the 32-point range light—"towing range lights." The towing range lights are more commonly used than the towing masthead lights in inland waters. In the Inland Rules, the two 12-point amber pushing lights are displayed at the stern only if pushing ahead *and* displaying towing masthead lights.

A *vessel engaged in fishing* is recognized by distinctive red over white 32-point lights. No other lights are shown in inland waters.

The *steam pilot vessel* under the Inland Rules is required to show white over red 32-point lights at the masthead and sidelights when not at anchor. The Inland Rules also require a flare-up light to be shown at maximum intervals of 15 minutes. Pilot vessels at anchor are required to show the white over red lights in lieu of anchor lights.

A *vessel at anchor* shows only one light in inland waters if less than 150 feet in length. A vessel of 150 feet or upward in length is required to show two white lights. A vessel made fast to another vessel must maintain her own proper anchor lights.[1] A vessel moored at the end of a pier should display a light.[2]

The Inland Rules make no mention of a *vessel aground*; the International lights and shapes cannot be shown, since they have different meanings under the Pilot Rules. A vessel aground in inland waters must show the lights and shapes required for a vessel at anchor.[3] In order to warn approach-ing vessels, the danger signal of four or more short blasts, or the signals to attract attention (Article 12) should be used. Vessels requiring assistance should use the distress signals which are defined in Article 31.

Minesweeping is not specifically mentioned in the Inland Rules. The Pilot Rules provide for lights and shapes to be shown by a vessel towing a submerged or partly submerged object (Section 80.18).

Vessels in the following categories are not mentioned in the Inland Rules or Pilot Rules, and there are no special lights or shapes which may be shown in inland waters:

Vessel not under command
Vessel engaged in a towing operation such as renders her unable to deviate from her course
Vessel engaged in underway replenishment
Vessel launching or recovering aircraft
Vessel constrained by her draft.

MISCELLANEOUS PROVISIONS FOR INLAND WATERS

Distress Signals

Art. 31 When a vessel is in distress and requires assistance from other vessels or from the shore the following shall be the signal to be used or displayed by her, either together or separately, namely:

In the daytime—

A continuous sounding with any fog-signal apparatus, or firing a gun.

At night—

First. Flames on the vessel as from a burning tar barrel, oil barrel, and so forth.

Second. A continuous sounding with any fog-signal apparatus, or firing a gun.

1. The *Prudence*, D.C. Va. 1912, 197 F. 479.
2. The *Millville*, D.C.N.J. 1905, 137 F. 974.
3. The *Ant*, D.C.N.J. 1882, 10 F. 294.

The majority of the distress signals from the International Rules are accepted by custom in inland waters.

Signals to Attract Attention

Art. 12 Every vessel may, if necessary, in order to attract attention, in addition to the lights which she is required by these rules to carry, show a flare-up light or use any detonating signal that cannot be mistaken for a distress signal.

Lights on U.S. Naval Vessels and Coast Guard Cutters (in inland waters)

Art. 30 The exhibition of any light on board of a vessel of war of the United States or a Coast Guard cutter may be *suspended* whenever, in the opinion of the Secretary of the Navy, the commander in chief of a squadron, or the commander of a vessel acting singly, the special character of the service may require it.

If running "darkened ship" as permitted by Article 30, lights must still be exhibited in sufficient time to prevent collision. The primary reason for this provision is to protect against loss of vessels to enemy submarines in time of war. The purpose is defeated if military vessels are lost in collisions with friendly vessels.

Naval Lights and Recognition Signals

Art. 13 Nothing in these rules shall interfere with the operation of any special rules made by the Government of any nation with respect to *additional* station and signal lights for two or more ships of war or for vessels sailing under convoy, or with the exhibition of recognition signals adopted by shipowners, which have been authorized by their respective Governments, and duly registered and published.

Military Vessels of Special Construction or Purpose

Under the authority of International Rule 1(e), the United States has passed laws authorizing the Secretary of the Navy and the Secretary of Transportation to exempt Navy and Coast Guard vessels of special construction from certain requirements pertaining to lights.[4] The Coast Guard exceptions are published in Title 33, Code of Federal Regulations, Part 135. Light waivers for naval vessels are published in Title 32, Code of Federal Regulations, Part 706. Such exceptions are reproduced in CG-169.

Rule 1(e) of the International Rules provides:

Whenever the Government concerned shall have determined that a vessel of special construction or purpose cannot comply fully with the provisions of any of these rules with respect to the number, position, range or arc of visibility of lights or shapes, as well as to the disposition and characteristics of sound-signalling appliances, without interfering with the special function of the vessel, such vessel shall comply with such other provisions in regard to the number, position, range or arc of visibility of lights or shapes, as well as to the disposition and characteristics of sound-signalling appliances, as her Government shall have determined to be the closest possible compliance with these rules in respect to that vessel.

Submarines

U.S. Naval submarines are required to display an intermittent flashing amber (yellow) beacon with a

4. 33 USC 1052 and 33 USC 360.

sequential operation of one flash per second for 3 seconds, followed by a 3-second off period. The light will be shone in addition to the others prescribed for submarines, and displayed in inland and international waters.

Barges Pushed Ahead

A 20-point flashing amber light (50 to 70 flashes per minute) is displayed on the Gulf Coast and Gulf Intracoastal Waterway at the forward end of a tow being pushed ahead. This applies when one or more barges, canalboats, scows, or other vessels of nondescript type not otherwise provided for, are being towed by pushing ahead, or by a combination of pushing ahead and towing alongside. Pilot Rules, Section 80.16(a).

Law Enforcement Vessels

A rotating blue light may be used by law enforcement vessels in addition to the other prescribed lights and shapes. Pilot Rules, Section 80.45.

Ferryboats

In addition to sidelights, double-end ferryboats are required to carry two 32-point range lights at the same height. Another light may be shown above the range lights for the purpose of distinguishing different ferryboat lines from each other. Pilot Rules, Section 80.15.

Lights for Small Vessels in Bad Weather

Whenever vessels of less than ten gross tons cannot display fixed sidelights in bad weather, a single lantern showing red on the port side and green on the starboard side will be exhibited in time to prevent collision. Inland Rules, Article 6.

Rowing Boats

Rowing boats, whether under oars or sail, shall have ready at hand a lantern showing a white light which shall be temporarily exhibited in sufficient time to prevent collision. Inland Rules, Article 7.

Lights for Barges, Canalboats, Scows, and Other Nondescript Vessels

See the Pilot Rules as follows:
Atlantic and Pacific coasts ...... Section 80.16
Gulf Coast and Gulf Intra-
    coastal Waterway .... Section 80.16(a)
Hudson River and Lake
    Champlain .... Section 80.17
Vessels operating temporarily on waters
requiring different lights ... Section 80.16(b)

Lights for Rafts and Other Craft Not Provided for

See Pilot Rules, Section 80.32.

Operating Under Bridges

Any vessel while passing under a bridge may temporarily lower any lights or shapes when required to do so because of the restricted vertical clearance under the bridge, but they shall be exhibited as required by law or regulation immediately when clear of the bridge. Pilot Rules, Section 80.40.

Blinding Lights

Flashing the rays of a searchlight or other blinding light onto the bridge or into the pilot house of any vessel underway is prohibited. Pilot Rules, Section 80.34.

Lights, Whistles, and Bells for Motorboats Not More Than 65 Feet in Length

See Appendix D.

3 Responsibilities Between Vessels — Right of Way

This chapter is concerned primarily with the right of way between different categories of vessels, namely:

Steam vessels—including pilot vessels and steam vessels engaged in towing or pushing, but not engaged in fishing

Sailing vessels—vessels under sail only and not engaged in fishing

Vessels engaged in fishing—regardless of means of propulsion.

The rules that pertain to a sailing vessel approaching another sailing vessel will also be given at the end of this chapter. The rules that apply to a steam vessel approaching another steam vessel will appear in later chapters.

The discussion of right of way between vessels will be limited to vessels underway, as the presumption of fault will be against a moving vessel in cases where a moving vessel collides with a vessel which is not underway (or with a vessel which is underway and not moving). In some cases, however, the vessel not underway may be found at fault for improper lights, or for improper position. The circumstances may dictate that a vessel at anchor must have an anchor watch in order that some warning can be given in addition to the anchor lights, or to protect against the possibility of dragging. A vessel anchored in fog was liable for 20 percent of the damages for her failure to keep her engines on standby and to let go the anchor chain to avoid collision. These precautions were necessary because the traffic and fog made the situation particularly hazardous and the vessel was not anchored in a charted anchorage area.[1] A typical court opinion in a 1962 case stated:

Where a moving vessel collides with an anchored vessel, burden is upon moving vessel to exonerate herself from the blame by showing that it was not within her power to have avoided the collision by

1. *Getty Oil Co., Inc.* v. *S.S. Ponce DeLeon*, C.A. N.Y. 1977, 555 F. 2d 328.

taking reasonable precautions, but such burden shifts where it appears that a contributing cause of collision was absence of statutory lights on the anchored vessel.[2]

Whenever two or three red lights in a vertical line are seen with no masthead or range light in inland waters, the lights indicate a vessel which is not moving and which must be avoided. In the case of a floating plant in a channel, it may be necessary to stop and wait for the channel to be cleared.

BURDENED AND PRIVILEGED DUTIES

Whenever two vessels are approaching each other, at least one of them is required to keep out of the way of the other. A vessel required to maneuver is a *burdened* vessel, and may be required to change course, change speed, or both, in order to keep out of the way of the other vessel. In some situations, both vessels are burdened. The duties of the burdened vessel are given in Inland Rules, Article 22 and 23:

> **Art. 22** Every vessel which is directed by these rules to keep out of the way of another vessel shall, if the circumstances of the case admit, avoid crossing ahead of the other.

> **Art. 23** Every steam vessel which is directed by these rules to keep out of the way of another vessel shall, on approaching her, if necessary, slacken her speed or stop or reverse.

The phrase "if the circumstances of the case admit" in Article 22 can be interpreted to mean that it is a definite requirement to avoid crossing ahead of the other vessel, unless it is necessary to

2. *Willis* v. *Tugs Tramp and Mars*, D.C. Va. 1962, 216 F. Supp. 901.

avoid immediate danger caused by some peril other than the approaching vessel.

If two vessels are approaching in a situation such that only one is burdened, the other vessel is *privileged*. The duty of the privileged vessel is given in Inland Rules, Article 21:

> Where, by any of these rules, one of the two vessels is to keep out of the way, the other shall keep her course and speed.

The purpose of the requirement to maintain course and speed permits the burdened vessel to know with certainty what the privileged vessel will do. With the knowledge that the privileged vessel will maintain course and speed, the burdened vessel can plan her maneuver.

Overtaking Vessel

A vessel of any category is always burdened when overtaking another vessel. No whistle signals will be sounded unless *both* vessels are steam vessels (the overtaking situation between two steam vessels is discussed in Chapter 4).

Sailing Vessel

Article 20 of the Inland Rules gives sailing vessels the right of way over steam vessels:

> **Art. 20** When a steam vessel and a sailing vessel are proceeding in such directions as to involve risk of collision, the steam vessel shall keep out of the way of the sailing vessel. This rule shall not give to a sailing vessel the right to hamper, in a narrow channel, the safe passage of a steam vessel which can navigate only inside that channel.

Fishing Vessel

Vessels engaged in fishing have the right of way over sailing vessels:

Art. 26. Sailing vessels under way shall keep out of the way of sailing vessels or boats fishing with nets, lines, or trawls. This rule shall not give to any vessel or boat engaged in fishing the right of obstructing a fairway used by vessels other than fishing vessels or boats.

A vessel engaged in fishing is prohibited from obstructing a fairway used by vessels other than fishing vessels (a fairway is not limited to the channel, but includes all navigable waters where vessels habitually move). The Inland Rules do not give a fishing vessel the right of way over a steam vessel, but a federal district court construed Articles 20 and 26 together to give the right of way to the fishing vessel. This decision was upheld by a federal court of appeals:

> The trial judge found that the maneuver in the present case was not an ordinary "overtaking." The Liberty II was a vessel engaged in fishing, and the Inland Rules require that a sailing vessel keep out of the way of such a fishing vessel. Further, the Inland Rules require steam vessels to keep out of the way of sailing vessels. Therefore, the trial judge reasoned, a steam vessel must keep out of the way of a fishing vessel. We find no fault with this conclusion. Even absent this finding of the trial judge regarding the status of steam and fishing vessels, expert testimony at trial indicated that it was the custom of steam vessels to keep out of the way of fishing vessels.[3]

Other Categories of Vessels

The following vessels were mentioned in an earlier chapter as having no special lights or shapes in inland waters of the United States:

---

3. *Pinto* v. *M/S Fernwood*, C.C.A., 1974, 507 F. 2d 1327.

Vessel not under command
Vessel engaged in a towing operation such as renders her unable to deviate from her course
Vessel engaged in underway replenishment
Vessel launching or recovering aircraft
Vessel constrained by her draft.

A vessel not under command is a vessel which is unable to maneuver because of a steering casualty, loss of suction, or some other cause. No mention is made of a vessel not under command in Inland or Pilot Rules, but the courts require a vessel in such a situation to use the inland danger signal of four or more short blasts on the whistle to warn other vessels of her inability to abide by the rules.[4] A vessel engaged in a towing operation such as renders her unable to deviate from her course should make the same use of the danger signal.

The Inland Rules and Pilot Rules make no mention of vessels engaged in underway replenishment or launching and recovering aircraft. Vessels so engaged must adhere to the duties of a burdened vessel when required by the rules prescribing right of way. Such activities should be suspended, if possible, until located in international waters.

A vessel constrained by her draft, while having no special lights or shapes, is given the right of way over vessels which are more maneuverable. Steam vessels less than 65 feet in length and sailing vessels must not hamper a steam vessel in a channel if the larger vessel can navigate only inside that channel.

A vessel engaged in minesweeping can show the lights and shapes for a vessel with a submerged tow, but such a vessel is not given the right of way in inland waters.

---

4. *Tiger Shipping Co., S. A.* v. *Tug Carville*, D.C. Va. 1974, 381 F. Supp. 1340.

SUMMARY OF RIGHT-OF-WAY PROVISIONS IN THE INLAND RULES

Steam vessel must keep out of the way of a *sailing vessel.*

Sailing vessel must keep out of the way of a *vessel engaged in fishing.*

Court interpretation: *Steam vessel* must keep out of the way of a *vessel engaged in fishing.*

Steam vessels less than 65 feet in length and *sailing vessels* must keep out of the way of a large *steam vessel restricted to a channel.*

Vessel engaged in fishing must not obstruct a fairway.

Notwithstanding the right of way between the above categories, an overtaking vessel must keep out of the way of a vessel overtaken.

RIGHT OF WAY — SAILING VESSEL APPROACHING SAILING VESSEL

Inland Rules, Article 17:

When two sailing vessels are approaching each other so as to involve risk of collision, one of them shall keep out of the way of the other as follows, namely:

(a) A vessel which is running free shall keep out of the way of a vessel which is closehauled.

(b) A vessel which is closehauled on the port tack shall keep out of the way of a vessel which is closehauled on the starboard tack.

(c) When both are running free, with the wind on different sides, the vessel which has the wind on the port side shall keep out of the way of the other.

(d) When both are running free, with the wind on the same side, the vessel which is to windward shall keep out of the way of the vessel which is to leeward.

(e) A vessel which has the wind aft shall keep out of the way of the other vessel.

CLOSEHAULED (beating)—wind from direction within 5 points (approximately) of dead ahead. When the average boat sails with the wind broad on her bow, she is beating.

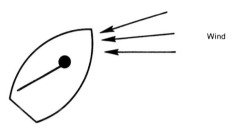

WIND AFT (running before the wind)—wind from direction within 2 points of dead astern.

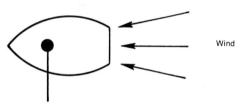

RUNNING FREE (includes close reach, beam reach, and broad reach)—wind from direction between 5 points aft the bow to 2 points forward of the stern.

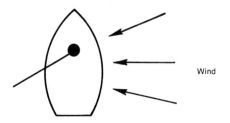

4 Approach Situations Between Steam Vessels in Sight

In Chapter 3 the right of way between different categories of vessels—steam vessel, sailing vessel, and vessel engaged in fishing—was discussed, as well as the right of way between two sailing vessels. The right of way between sailing vessels was determined by point of sail (relative direction of wind) and tack (whether the wind is over the port of starboard side). The privileged or burdened status of two steam vessels approaching each other is determined by the approach situation—overtaking, meeting, or crossing. Two conditions are necessary before any of the three approach situations can exist between two steam vessels:

1. There must be a risk of collision.
2. The vessels must be in sight of each other.

RISK OF COLLISION

The preliminary to the inland steering and sailing rules states:

Risk of collision can, when circumstances permit, be ascertained by carefully watching the compass bearing of an approaching vessel. If the bearing does not appreciably change, such risk should be deemed to exist.

There can be no hard-and-fast rule which prescribes a rate-of-bearing change by which risk of collision can be determined. Bearings will change at different rates for vessels at different ranges from each other. The one conclusion that can be made is that taking bearings on an approaching vessel is a requirement of the rules. It is important that the bearings be compass bearings (true or magnetic), since relative bearings provide no useful information when heading is changed. If the true bearing of a vessel remains nearly constant, and the range is decreasing, the two vessels are on a collision course. When the true bearings are changing rapidly, the bearings will show the side on which the other vessel will pass, providing both vessels maintain course and speed. If the bearing is increasing numerically, a vessel on the starboard hand will pass astern, a vessel on the port hand will cross ahead. If the bearing is decreasing numerically, a vessel on the starboard hand will cross ahead, a vessel on the port hand will pass astern.

The meaning of *risk of collision* has been expanded by the courts:

> Risk of collision begins the very moment when the two vessels have approached so near each other and upon such courses, that by a departure from the rules of navigation, whether from want of good seamanship, accident, mistake, misapprehension of signals, or otherwise, a collision might be brought about. It is true, that, prima facie, each has a right to assume that the other will obey the law. But this does not justify either in shutting his eyes to what the other may actually do, or in omitting to do what he can to avoid an accident, made imminent by the acts of the other. I say the right above is prima facie merely because it is known that departures from the law not only may, but do, take place, and often. Risk of collision may be said to begin the moment the two vessels have approached so near that a collision might be brought about by any such departure, and continues up to the moment when they have so far progressed that no such result could ensue . . . . The idea that there was no risk of collision is fully exploded by the fact that there was a collision.[1]

VESSELS IN SIGHT

The meeting, overtaking, and crossing situations apply only to vessels in sight, which does not include tracking by radar. The situations apply in fog and other conditions of restricted visibility, *but only after the vessels have sighted each other.* The

1. The *Milwaukee*, 1871, Fed. Cas. No. 9, 626.

above provisions are found in Inland Rules, Article 18, where the one- and two-short-blast signals are discussed:

> The whistle signals provided in the rules under this article, for steam vessels meeting, passing, or overtaking, are never to be used except when steamers are in sight of each other, and the course and position of each can be determined in the day time by a sight of the vessel itself, or by night by seeing its signal lights. In fog, mist, falling snow or heavy rainstorms, when vessels can not see each other, fog signals only must be given.

Note that the one- and two-short-blast signals are given only when two *steam* vessels are approaching each other. A steam vessel approaching a sailing vessel would sound no signals.

Section 80.03 of the Pilot Rules contains the following statements: "one short blast of the whistle signifies intention to direct course to own starboard"; "two short blasts of the whistle signify intention to direct course to own port." The two statements are in conflict with the Inland Rules which govern the meeting and overtaking situations, and are therefore invalid. The one- and two-short-blast signals are signals of proposal—agreement in the meeting and overtaking situations. The Inland Rules prescribe no signals for the crossing situation, which will be discussed in some detail later in this chapter.

BACKING SIGNAL

The backing signal is given by a steam vessel when a vessel of any category is in sight. Both Article 28 of the Inland Rules and Section 80.03(b) of the Pilot Rules state:

> When vessels are in sight of one another a steam vessel underway whose engines are going full

speed astern shall indicate that fact by three short blasts on the whistle.

Court interpretations of the requirement for the backing signal have effectively changed the meaning to "my engines are going astern (at any speed) *or* I have sternway on." In one case a vessel was found at fault for not repeating her three-blast signal when the action of the other vessel indicated that it had not been heard; the circumstances required that the backing signal be given when the engines were stopped while the vessel had sternway.[2] In another case a vessel was required to give the backing signal when twisting with slight sternway — one engine was going ahead and the other was reversing at reduced speed.[3]

DANGER SIGNAL

Article 18 of the Inland Rules and Section 80.1 of the Pilot Rules state:

If, when steam vessels are approaching each other, either vessel fails to understand the course or intention of the other, from any cause, the vessel so in doubt shall immediately signify the same by giving several short and rapid blasts, not less than four, of the steam whistle.

While the one-, two- and three-short-blast signals are to be used only by vessels in sight, the courts have ruled that the danger signal may be required in fog.[4]

2. The *Sicilian Prince*, C.C.A.N.Y. 1905, 144 F. 951.
3. The *Deutschland*, C.C.A.N.Y. 1904, 137 F. 1018; 129 F. 964.
4. The *Virginian*, C.C.A. Wash. 1916, 238 F. 156. The Celtic Monarch, D.C. Wash. 1910, 175 F. 1006.

CROSS SIGNALS

Section 80.2 of the Pilot Rules states:

Steam vessels are forbidden to use what has become technically known among pilots as "cross signals," that is, answering one whistle with two, and answering two whistles with one.

BURDENED AND PRIVILEGED DUTIES

The Inland Rules governing the above duties are:

Art. 21 Where, by any of these rules, one of the two vessels is to keep out of the way, the other shall keep her course and speed.

Art. 22 Every vessel which is directed by these rules to keep out of the way of another vessel shall, if the circumstances of the case admit, avoid crossing ahead of the other.

Art. 23 Every steam vessel which is directed by these rules to keep out of the way of another vessel shall, on approaching her, if necessary, slacken her speed or stop or reverse.

VESSEL BRIDGE-TO-BRIDGE RADIOTELEPHONE ACT

This law went into effect on 1 January 1973, and is an important step toward the prevention of collisions in inland waters (it also applies to the Great Lakes and Western Rivers). It requires the following vessels to guard the frequency 156.65 MHz for bridge-to-bridge communications:

1. Power-driven (steam) vessels of 300 gross tons and upward.
2. Vessels of 100 gross tons and upward that are for hire and carry one or more passengers.

3. Commercial towing vessels of 26 feet or over in length.
4. Manned dredges and floating plants working in or near a channel or fairway.

The radiotelephone frequency is for the exclusive use of the person in charge of the vessel, who shall, when necessary, *transmit and confirm the intentions of his vessel and any other information necessary for the safe navigation of vessels.* Even when not transmitting, guarding the frequency can be invaluable in appraising a traffic situation; knowledge of the intentions of other vessels is added to what is ordinarily observed by radar or visual means, or the signals of vessels within range of hearing.

The primary advantage of the bridge-to-bridge radiotelephone is gained when communication between two vessels results in agreement on their intentions in a situation which might have ended in collision because of misunderstanding and confusion. In the following discussion on the three approach situations, keep in mind that signals are not always heard, and are often misinterpreted when only part of the signal is heard (one blast heard when two were sounded, etc.). This writer recommends that whenever the course or intention of another vessel is not *immediately* understood, communication should be established on the bridge-to-bridge frequency. In this way, intentions may be confirmed early, and the misunderstandings which would require the sounding of the danger signal would be avoided. Regardless of the information exchanged, nothing in the Radiotelephone Act "relieves any person from the obligation of complying with the rules of the road and applicable pilot rules."

Section 83.251 of the regulations issued by the Federal Communications Commission requires transmissions similar to the following format:

THIS IS THE (name of vessel). MY POSITION IS (give readily identifiable position and, if useful, course and speed) ABOUT TO (describe contemplated action). OUT.

VESSEL OFF (give a readily identifiable position). THIS IS (name of vessel) OFF (give a readily identifiable position). I PLAN TO (give proposed course of action). OVER.

Vessels acknowledging receipt shall answer:

(Name of vessel calling). THIS IS (name of vessel answering). RECEIVED YOUR CALL (follow with an indication of intentions). Communications shall terminate when each ship is satisfied that the other no longer poses a threat to its safety and is ended with "OUT."

See Appendix A for log-keeping requirements.

OVERTAKING SITUATION

The rules governing the overtaking situation appear in Articles 18 and 24 of the Inland Rules and Section 80.6 of the Pilot Rules:

When steam vessels are running in the same direction, and the vessel which is astern shall desire to pass on the right or starboard hand of the vessel ahead, she shall give one short blast of the steam whistle, as a signal of such desire, and if the vessel ahead answers with one blast, she shall direct her course to starboard; or if she shall desire to pass to the left or port side of the vessel ahead, she shall give two short blasts of the steam whistle as a signal of such desire, and if the vessel ahead answers with two blasts, shall direct her course to port; or if the vessel ahead does not think it safe for the vessel astern to attempt to pass at that point, she shall immediately signify the same by

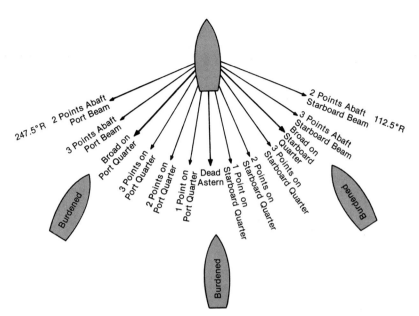

Fig. 29 Overtaking situation:

giving several short and rapid blasts of the steam whistle, not less than four, and under no circumstances shall the vessel astern attempt to pass the vessel ahead until such time as they have reached a point where it can be safely done, when said vessel shall signify her willingness by blowing the proper signals. The vessel ahead shall in no case attempt to cross the bow or crowd upon the course of the passing vessel.

As by day the overtaking vessel cannot always know with certainty whether she is forward of or abaft this direction from the other vessel she should, if in doubt, assume that she is an overtaking vessel and keep out of the way.

Every vessel coming up with another vessel from any direction more than two points abaft her beam, that is, in such a position with reference to the vessel which she is overtaking that she would be unable to see either of that vessel's sidelights, shall be deemed to be an overtaking vessel; and no subsequent alteration of the bearing between the two vessels shall make the overtaking vessel a crossing vessel within the meaning of the rules in this part, or relieve her of the duty of keeping clear of the overtaken vessel until she is finally past and clear.

The rules which apply to the overtaking situation are the most clear-cut of the three approach situations. The situation applies when vessels are heading generally in the same direction with the vessel behind going faster than the vessel ahead. A vessel is overtaking if approaching the vessel ahead from more than two points abaft her beam. If there is any doubt that a vessel is forward or abaft this direction from the vessel ahead, she should assume that she is overtaking. At night a vessel overtaking another would be unable to see either sidelight of the vessel ahead.

The overtaking vessel is burdened. If she desires to overtake on the starboard side of the vessel ahead, she sounds one short blast. If she desires to overtake on the port side of the vessel ahead, she sounds two short blasts. The overtaking vessel is not permitted to pass the vessel ahead until the overtaken vessel answers with the same signal.

The overtaken vessel is privileged, and is required to promptly answer the proposal of the overtaking vessel. If she agrees to the proposal she answers with the same signal. If she does not agree to the signal, because of an obvious danger ahead or her own plans to make a maneuver, she must immediately answer with the danger signal. The privileged vessel is not obligated to maintain course and speed until she agrees to the proposal of the overtaking vessel.[5] The privileged vessel is legally maintaining course and speed when maneuvering to follow the turns of a channel or to avoid immediate dangers such as rocks or shoals. Such maneuvers must be anticipated by the overtaking vessel. The overtaken vessel may ease to give the passing vessel more room, but is not required to do so.

When the first signal of the overtaking vessel is answered with the danger signal, the overtaken vessel can subsequently indicate by one or two short blasts when it is safe to pass, or the overtaking vessel can initiate a new proposal. "The signal of an overtaking vessel must be repeated if not responded to, and the possibility of collision avoided, if necessary, by slackening speed and changing course."[6]

5. The *Industry*, C.C.A.N.Y. 1928, 29 F. 2d 29.
6. *Ervin* v. *Neversink Steamboat Co.*, 1882, 88 N.Y. 184.

The courts have generally ruled that the overtaking vessel must signal if she will approach the vessel ahead so close that a sudden change of course by the latter would bring about a collision. The so-called "half-mile rule" from paragraph 80.3(a) of the Pilot Rules has not been applied by the courts to the overtaking situation. Nevertheless, it is wise never to omit signals if the closest point of approach (CPA) is less than half a mile.

A common cause of collisions in the overtaking situation is the suction which draws two ships together. The force of suction is greatest when the overtaking vessel is passing at a high relative speed in shallow water, and particularly when the overtaken vessel is close aboard a deep-draft vessel on one side and a bank on the other.

The discussions in this chapter relate to situations where a steam vessel is approaching another steam vessel. If one of the two vessels in an overtaking situation is a sailing vessel, no signals will be exchanged.

MEETING SITUATIONS

Head and Head

The meeting situation is defined primarily by the sighting of the other vessel's sidelights rather than by relative direction in points. Article 18 and Section 80.4 of the Pilot Rules both state in part:

> When steam vessels are approaching each other head and head, that is, end on, or nearly so, it shall be the duty of each to pass on the port side of the other, and either vessel shall give, as a signal of her intention one short and distinct blast of her whistle, which the other vessel shall answer promptly

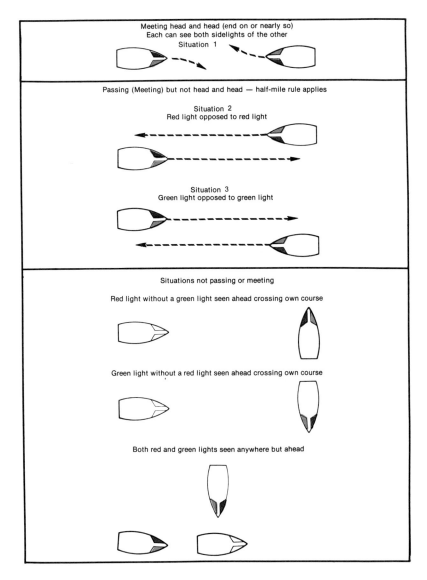

Meeting head and head (end on or nearly so)
Each can see both sidelights of the other
Situation 1

Passing (Meeting) but not head and head — half-mile rule applies

Situation 2
Red light opposed to red light

Situation 3
Green light opposed to green light

Situations not passing or meeting

Red light without a green light seen ahead crossing own course

Green light without a red light seen ahead crossing own course

Both red and green lights seen anywhere but ahead

Fig. 30 Meeting situations.

by a similar blast of her whistle, and thereupon such vessels shall pass on the port side of each other . . . . The foregoing only applies to cases where vessels are meeting end on or nearly end on, in such a manner as to involve risk of collision; in other words, to cases in which, by day, each vessel sees the masts of the other in a line, or nearly in a line, with her own, and by night to cases in which each vessel is in such a position as to see both the sidelights of the other.

Since you do not know if the other vessel can see both your sidelights, a situation is generally considered to be head and head if both sidelights of the other (or masts in line or nearly in line) are seen within approximately one point of the bow (headings within two points of being opposite). If doubt exists in a situation which is borderline between meeting and crossing, it is prudent to assume that it is a meeting situation (when holding a vessel approximately one point on the port bow, it would be dangerous to assume that you were privileged in a crossing situation). The head-and-head approach is shown in Figure 30 as Situation 1.

When meeting head and head, both vessels are burdened. One vessel proposes a port-to-port passage by sounding one short blast. The other vessel should answer promptly with one short blast, and both are required to alter course to starboard in order to pass port to port. This is the procedure required whenever the vessels cannot pass safely without altering course, even if they are slightly to starboard of each other.

Not Meeting Head and Head

Article 18 and Section 80.4 also state:

But if the courses of such vessels are so far to the starboard of each other as not to be considered as meeting head and head, either vessel shall immediately give two short and rapid blasts of her whistle, which the other vessel shall answer promptly by two similar blasts of her whistle, and they shall pass on the starboard side of each other.

Notice that this description fits Situation 3 shown in Figure 30, but Article 18 and Section 80.4 conclude by saying:

[The foregoing] does not apply by day to cases in which a vessel sees another ahead crossing her own course, or by night to cases where the red light of one vessel is opposed to the red light of the other, or where the green light of one vessel is opposed to the green light of the other, or where a red light without a green light or a green light without a red light is seen ahead, or where both green and red lights are seen anywhere but ahead.

The above makes no provision for Situation 2, and might also seem to eliminate Situation 3 which was provided for earlier. The problem is resolved by the so-called "half-mile rule," which appears only in the Pilot Rules, Section 80.3(a):

The signals for passing, by the blowing of the whistle, shall be given and answered by pilots . . . not only when meeting "head and head," or nearly so, but at all times when the steam vessels are in sight of each other, when *passing or meeting* at a distance within half a mile of each other, and whether passing to starboard or port. [Emphasis added.]

The half-mile rule does not apply to the overtaking and crossing situations.

A district court, in upholding the half-mile rule in a case involving a starboard-to-starboard meeting which was not meeting "head and head," noted the need to resolve the validity of the rule, and concluded:

The rule does purport to require signals whenever the projected course of the vessels will bring them within one-half mile of each other, regardless of whether they are end on or nearly so. The rule as construed is not inconsistent with the statutory rule . . . . It does not contradict the statutory rule, but merely supplements it.[7]

Note that in both Situation 2 (passing port to port) and Situation 3 (passing starboard to starboard) the vessels would pass clear if they remained on their courses. If the projected courses would bring them within one-half mile of each other (CPA within one-half mile) signals must be exchanged.

Maneuvering in the Meeting Situations

In a meeting situation, course should not be altered until the approaching vessel answers the proposal with the same signal (one or two short blasts), unless to avoid immediate danger.[8] (Keep in mind that a port-to-port passage is required when within the definition of meeting head and head.) If the other vessel crosses your signal, or makes a proposal with which you do not agree, the courts require that you sound the danger signal and stop your engines, and reverse if the proximity of the vessels requires it.[9] A vessel which answers two short blasts with the danger signal, and then sounds one short blast without stopping or reversing, is guilty of cross signals — even if the original

7. *Compania Carreto De Navigation, S.A.* v. *Tug Sagamore*, D.C.N.Y. 1963, 223 F. Supp. 598.

8. *Moore-McCormack Lines, Inc.* v. *S. S. Portmar*, D.C.N.Y. 1966, 249 F. Supp. 464 (head and head). In re Pacific Far East Line, Inc., D.C.Cal 1970, 314 F. Supp. 1339 (starboard-to-starboard meeting).

9. The *Fulton*, C.C.A.N.Y. 1931, 54 F. 2d 467.

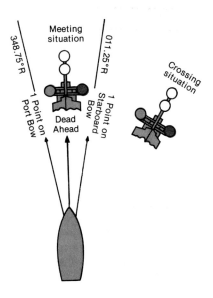

Fig. 31 Crossing v. meeting.

proposal was an improper one. After stopping, signals must be exchanged before the vessels pass each other.

If a vessel does not answer your proposal, the best procedure is not to repeat the signal, but follow the same procedure outlined above — sound the danger signal and stop, until signals for passing with safety have been exchanged and understood.

Backing Signal

In a meeting situation, with the vessels in visual sight, any time either vessel puts her engines astern at any speed, she must sound three short blasts.

Meeting in Restricted Waters

Article 25 of the Inland Rules and Section 80.10 of the Pilot Rules provide that:

> In narrow channels every steam vessel shall, when it is safe and practicable, keep to that side of the fairway or midchannel which lies on the starboard side of such vessel.

Therefore, if vessels are keeping to the right, passage should normally be port to port for vessels meeting in restricted waters. The courts have also held that:

> In determining how vessels are approaching each other, in narrow tortuous channels like the one here in question, the general course in the channel must alone be considered, and not the course they may be on by the compass at any particular time while pursuing the windings and turnings of the channel.[10]

10. The *Milwaukee*, 1871, Fed. Cas. No. 9, 626.

CROSSING SITUATIONS

The actions and signals required for the crossing situation have been the most confusing for the mariner. One reason is that the crossing situation is best defined by what it is *not*. A crossing situation is an approach situation between two steam vessels in visual sight, which is neither an overtaking nor a meeting situation.

Most students of the rules feel more comfortable with a definition that includes the relative bearing of the approaching vessel. Such a definition must satisfy all of the following requirements:

1. Vessel A holds vessel B in the arc between dead ahead and two points abaft the starboard beam.
2. Vessel B holds vessel A in the arc between dead ahead and two points abaft the port beam.
3. It is not a meeting situation.

Article 19 of the Inland Rules gives the basic requirement of the crossing situation:

> When two vessels are crossing, so as to involve risk of collision, the vessel which has the other on her own starboard side shall keep out of the way of the other.

The vessel that has the other on her own starboard hand is burdened in the crossing situation, and therefore must avoid crossing ahead of the privileged vessel, and if necessary, slacken her speed or stop or reverse. The privileged vessel is required to maintain course and speed.

It was mentioned earlier in this chapter that the Inland Rules prescribe no whistle signals for the crossing situation. The Pilot Rules provide a signal which may be sounded by the privileged vessel, as

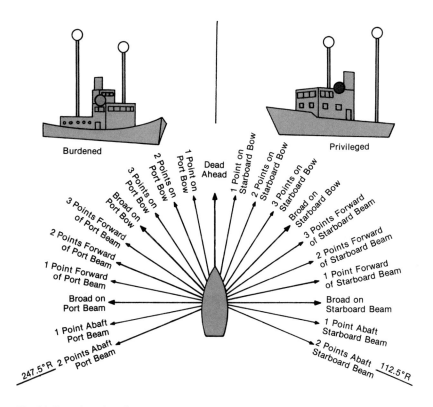

Fig. 32 Crossing situations.

well as other regulations to supplement Article 19. The court interpretations of these other regulations make the crossing situation one of the most complex aspects of the rules for inland waters. The following discussion describes the situation as currently interpreted by the courts.

Actions of the Privileged Vessel

Section 80.03(a) of the Pilot Rules says that "when two steam vessels are approaching each other at right angles or obliquely . . . one short blast of the whistle signifies intention . . . of steam vessel which is to starboard of the other to hold course and speed." The courts have held that this signal is not required but permissive:

> Privileged vessel, which was in plain sight in crossing courses situation, was not under duty to give passing signal and burdened vessel was not entitled to receive any signal.[11]

The courts do not require the privileged vessel to initiate a one-short-blast signal, nor will she be found at fault for failure to answer the burdened vessel's signal of one short blast.[12] A little reflection would indicate that this interpretation does not indicate the best procedure to follow in many situations. The privileged vessel in many cases may alert the burdened vessel to her duty when she sounds her intention to maintain course and speed. If the burdened vessel initiates the signal, it would seem to be good seamanship for the privileged vessel to answer, if for no other reason than to provide reassurance to the burdened vessel.

Although use of the one-blast signal by the privileged vessel is permissive — if the signal is given at all, it must be given in a timely manner. A privileged vessel was found at fault in one case for sounding the signal too late. The burdened vessel, who had not discovered the presence of the other, was a tug with tow who had no chance to maneuver out of the way after the signal of the privileged vessel. The burdened vessel was, of course, found at fault for failure to have a proper lookout. In finding the privileged vessel equally at fault, the court said:

> If signals are to be of any value, they must be given with an allowance of a sufficient time to exchange signals and agree on a passing, taking into consideration the speed, power and apparent agility of the vessels.[13]

The requirement for a privileged vessel in a crossing situation to maintain course and speed while the other vessel maneuvers to avoid collision can cause some anxious moments on the bridge. It is important to consider under what circumstances the privileged vessel should depart from that requirement in order to avoid a collision (under the provisions of the General Prudential Rule). The privileged vessel is required to maintain course and speed until in extremis. Since the term *in extremis* is not mentioned in the Inland Rules, we must turn to the courts for a definition:

> A steamer, when the privileged vessel, in crossing is not required to change course or reverse to avoid collision until it becomes evident that the other vessel will not or cannot keep out of the way.[14]

11. *Zim Israel Nav. Co.* v. *S.S. American Press*, D.C.N.Y. 1963, 222 F. Supp. 947.

12. Since it is customary for the burdened vessel also to give one short blast, its meaning might best be described as signalling intention to fulfill her obligations as the burdened vessel.

13. *River Terminals Corp.* v. *U.S.*, D.C. La. 1954, 121 F. Supp. 98.

14. The *Mary Powell*, N.Y. 1899, 92 F. 408.

It must be determined by the privileged vessel when this crucial point has been reached. The privileged vessel is required to maintain course and speed until in extremis — the privileged vessel stands on even when the burdened vessel does not signal or fails to answer a one-short-blast signal. The danger signal is required if the course or intention of the burdened vessel is in doubt. As will be seen later, the above provisions will be modified if either vessel sounds two short blasts.

Actions of the Burdened Vessel

The Inland Rules require that the burdened vessel avoid crossing ahead of the privileged vessel, and if necessary, slacken her speed or stop or reverse. Section 80.7 of the Pilot Rules requires the burdened vessel "to keep out of the way of the other by directing her course to starboard so as to cross the stern of the other steam vessel, or, if necessary to do so, slacken her speed or stop or reverse." The Pilot Rules thus eliminate the possibility of the burdened vessel avoiding the other by turning left without crossing ahead of the privileged vessel. This requirement of the Pilot Rules has been upheld in at least one court decision.[15]

The burdened vessel's duty to avoid crossing ahead of the other is absolute, with or without the one-short-blast signal from the privileged vessel. The burdened vessel must not delay her maneuver waiting for a signal from the other vessel.

The psychology of the crossing situation must be kept in mind by the burdened vessel in planning her maneuver. If she slows down to allow the privileged vessel to cross ahead, this may not be as

15. *Scully* v. *New Jersey Lighterage Co.*, C.C.A.N.Y. 1893, 58 F. 251.

readily apparent as turning smartly to starboard. A good guide is always to turn to starboard so as to point astern of the privileged vessel.

The burdened vessel is not specifically required by the rules to give a signal. It would seem to be good seamanship to answer a one-blast signal given by the privileged vessel. The burdened vessel may also initiate a one-short-blast signal.

Pilot Rules Modify Requirements of Privileged Vessel

The Inland Rules require that the privileged vessel maintain course and speed until in extremis. Section 80.7(b) of the Pilot Rules, quoted below, has modified that requirement; this modification was validated by a Supreme Court decision in 1940.[16]

> If from any causes the conditions covered by this situation are such as to prevent immediate compliance with each other's signals, the misunderstanding or objection shall be at once made apparent by blowing the danger signal, and both steam vessels shall be stopped and backed if necessary, until signals for passing with safety are made and understood.

According to the court interpretations discussed earlier, there is no "misunderstanding or objection" if one or both of the vessels fails to sound a one-short-blast signal, i.e., the privileged vessel is not relieved of her obligation to maintain course and speed, nor is the burdened vessel relieved of her

16. "We think that Inspectors' Rule II [Pilot Rules, Section 80.2] should be read in connection with their Rule VII [paragraph 80.7(b)] and that both should be construed in the light of the statutory provision in Article 27. . . . We hold these rules are not essentially inconsistent with the statute and are valid." *Postal S.S. Corp.* v. *Steamship El Isleo*, 1940, 84 L. Ed. 335.

obligation to avoid crossing ahead, merely because the other vessel does not sound one short blast. For the privileged vessel, there must be a more positive indication that the burdened vessel is not going to fulfill her obligations. When the burdened vessel shows by her maneuvers, or lack of maneuvers, that she "will not or cannot keep out of the way," the situation results in a maneuver in extremis.

The positive indications that are addressed by Section 80.7 of the Pilot Rules are *misunderstanding* and *objection*, which have been interpreted by the courts in the following manner:

Misunderstanding = cross signals

Objection = an unacceptable proposal.

The only case where a one-short-blast proposal might be unacceptable is when a burdened vessel finds herself unable to get out of the way due to "special circumstances." In such a situation, she would answer the privileged vessel's one-short-blast signal with the danger signal. The privileged vessel would then be required to stop her engines and, if the proximity of the vessels required it, back down. Before continuing the application of Section 80.7 to cases involving "cross signals" and "unacceptable proposals," the status of the two-short-blast signal in the crossing situation must be clarified.

It should be emphasized from the start that a signal of two short blasts in the crossing situation is illegal. There is nothing either expressed or implied in the Inland or Pilot Rules to justify a signal of two short blasts by *either* vessel. It is mentioned here only because it is a signal that may be heard, possibly in keeping with a local custom — a custom that may persist despite the fact that it is contrary to law.

A signal from the burdened vessel of two short blasts is a proposal to depart from the rules by crossing the bow of the privileged vessel. Because of the danger inherent in such a proposal, the privileged vessel is required to answer a signal of two short blasts.[17] The proposal is not binding on the privileged vessel, therefore the answer will normally be the danger signal of four or more short blasts. ("Special circumstances" may justify the privileged vessel in giving an answer of two short blasts — *see* Chapter 6.)

A two-short-blast signal from the privileged vessel may be considered as an offer to surrender her right of way to the burdened vessel. Such a proposal can be dismissed as being foolish — we are only considering here what to do when the *other* vessel initiates a two-blast signal.

With the status of the two-blast signal in mind, the application of Section 80.7 becomes more straightforward. As stated previously, the "misunderstanding" is caused by cross signals, defined in Section 80.2:

Steam vessels are forbidden to use what has become technically known among pilots as "cross signals," that is, answering one whistle with two, and answering two whistles with one.

If we sound one short blast, and the other vessel crosses our signal (answers with two short blasts), we are required by the "misunderstanding" *to sound the danger signal and stop.*

If the other vessel initiates a signal, and it is a proposal that is unacceptable, we are required by this "objection" to *sound the danger signal and stop.*

17. The *New York*, 1899, 20 S. Ct. 67.

If the other vessel sounds the danger signal, we are required to *stop* (it is not necessary to answer a danger signal with another danger signal).

Only after both vessels have at least stopped their engines (the proximity of the vessels may require that the vessels back down) will any more signals be sounded. At this point it is required that the vessels *exchange signals in agreement* before proceeding. They must first stop, and then exchange signals — they may not attempt to exchange signals while continuing to approach each other. As expressed by a circuit court of appeals, commenting on the 1940 Supreme Court decision mentioned earlier:

> There can be no doubt that the Supreme Court meant to hold that in a crossing case, when the holding-on vessel gets two blasts from the giving-way vessel, which are unacceptable to her, she must neither cross the signal, nor keep her speed, but must at least stop her engines, and if necessary back, "until signals for passing with safety are made and understood". . . . Rule VII [now Pilot Rules, Section 80.7(b)] is explicit; it forbids any agreement other than an assent to the proposal, until after the vessels have at least stopped their engines. They may not undertake to agree while they remain underway.[18]

Backing Signal

In a crossing situation, with the vessels in visual sight, any time either vessel puts her engines astern at any speed, including a maneuver in extremis, she must sound three short blasts.

18. *Postal S.S. Corp.* v. *Steamship El Isleo*, C.C.A. 1940, 112 F. 2d 297.

NARROW CHANNELS

Every steam vessel is required to keep to the right in a narrow channel. Therefore meeting vessels should normally pass port to port, and overtaking vessels pass to the port of the vessel ahead, when approaching in a narrow channel.

Steam vessels less than 65 feet in length, vessels engaged in fishing, and sailing vessels are not to hamper a vessel which can navigate only inside such a channel. Such a steam vessel should alert a small vessel of her duty with the danger signal, if it appears that the smaller vessel will get in the way. An overtaken vessel is still privileged, and a steam vessel must be prepared to slow down to the speed of the vessel ahead until the smaller vessel has an opportunity to get out of the way. Small vessels must also be alert to the danger posed by large vessels who may travel a great distance before a backing bell effectively reduces their headway.

Uses of Long-Blast Signal

Article 18, Rule V, of the Inland Rules and Section 80.5 of the Pilot Rules require two uses of the long-blast signal:

> (a) Whenever a steam vessel is nearing a short bend or curve in the channel, where, from the height of the banks or other cause, a steam vessel approaching from the opposite direction cannot be seen for a distance of half a mile, such steam vessel, when she shall have arrived within half a mile of such a curve or bend, shall give a signal by one long blast of the steam whistle, which signal shall be answered by a similar blast, given by any approaching steam vessel that may be within hearing. Should such signal be so answered by a

steam vessel upon the farther side of such bend, then the usual signals for meeting and passing shall immediately be given and answered; but, if the first alarm signal of such vessel be not answered, she is to consider the channel clear and govern herself accordingly.

(b) When steam vessels are moved from their docks or berths, and other boats are liable to pass from any direction toward them, they shall give the same signal as in the case of vessels meeting at a bend, but immediately after clearing the berths so as to be fully in sight they shall be governed by the steering and sailing rules.

In the first paragraph of Rule V describing the bend signal, "immediately" has been construed with Rule IX of Article 18 to mean that the one- or two-short-blast signals must be exchanged upon sighting each other after rounding the bend.

The signal for leaving a dock or berth is essentially an extension of the bend signal when the vessel is not in plain sight of approaching traffic. The signal is commonly called the "slip whistle" by the courts when so used, and it must be sounded repeatedly as long as the vessel is hidden from view. The signal is also required when the vessel moving from her dock or berth is in sight of other vessels.[19] The long-blast signal is not proper for a vessel who has been anchored or moored to a buoy while fully in sight of other vessels.

The courts have ruled that a vessel moving from her dock or berth is in "special circumstances" until settled on her course. Even in special circumstances, a backing vessel may signal her desire to cross ahead of an approaching vessel. The crossing rules do not apply, but by treating the stern of the backing vessel as the bow for the purpose of signals, she can make her desires known by one or two short blasts, depending on whether the approaching vessel is to the port or starboard of her "bow" (Figure 33, A and B). Such a signal is a proposal only; neither vessel is permitted or required by the rules to maintain course and speed.

A vessel which is backing in such a way that she is not crossing the course of another vessel is in a slightly different situation. She may be in a position where she is obstructing a channel or fairway while in the process of twisting toward her intended course. A vessel approaching from more than two points abaft her beam has been considered an overtaking vessel, even in cases where the twisting vessel was stopped in the water or making some sternway.

Figure 33 shows that a signal of two short blasts results in the approaching vessel leaving the backing vessel on her own starboard hand whether the backing vessel is crossing her course (situation A) or being overtaken (situation C). One short blast results in the backing vessel being left on the port hand in situations B and D.

The most common cause of collision involving a vessel leaving her slip with the proper signals is another vessel passing too near to pier ends at too great a speed.

Passing Floating Plant in Navigable Channels (Pilot Rules)

NOTE: The term "floating plant" as used in Sections 80.26 to 80.31a, includes dredges, derrick boats, snag boats, drill boats, pile drivers, maneuver boats, hydraulic graders, survey boats, working barges, and mat sinking plants.

19. *Grace Line, Inc.* v. *U.S. Lines Co.*, D.C.N.Y. 1961, 193 F. Supp. 664.

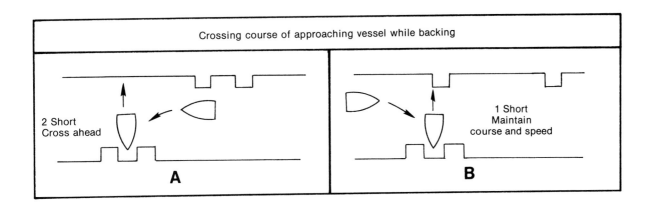

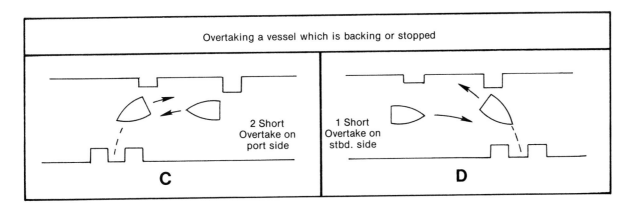

Fig. 33 Special circumstances involving a backing vessel.

Sec. 80.26 — Passing Signals.

(a) Vessels intending to pass dredges or other types of floating plant working in navigable channels, when within a reasonable distance therefrom and not in any case over a mile, shall indicate such intention by one long blast of the whistle, and shall be directed to the proper side for passage by the sounding, by the dredge or other floating plant, of the signal prescribed in the local pilot rules for vessels underway and approaching each other from opposite directions, which shall be answered in the usual manner by the approaching vessel.[20] If the channel is not clear, the floating plant shall sound the alarm or danger signal and the approaching vessel shall slow down or stop and await further signal from the plant.

(b) When the pipeline from a dredge crosses the channel in such a way that an approaching vessel cannot pass safely around the pipeline or dredge, there shall be sounded immediately from the dredge the alarm or danger signal and the approaching vessel shall slow down or stop and await further signal from the dredge. The pipeline shall then be opened and the channel cleared as soon as practicable; when the channel is clear for passage the dredge shall so indicate by sounding the usual passing signal as prescribed in paragraph (a) of this section. The approaching vessel shall answer with a corresponding signal and pass promptly.

(c) When any pipeline or swinging dredge shall have given an approaching vessel or tow the signal that the channel is clear, the dredge shall straighten out within the cut for the passage of the vessel or tow.

Sec. 80.27 — Speed of Vessels Passing Floating Plant Working in Channels.

Vessels, with or without tows, passing floating plant working in channels, shall reduce their speed sufficiently to insure the safety of both the plant and themselves, and when passing within 200 feet of the plant their speed shall not exceed five miles per hour.[21] While passing over lines of the plant, propelling machinery shall be stopped.

Sec. 80.28 — Light-draft Vessels Passing Floating Plant.

Vessels whose draft permits shall keep outside of the buoys marking the end of mooring lines of floating plant working in channels.

---

20. For example, if the floating plant sounds one short blast, the approaching vessel should answer with one short blast and leave the plant on her port hand.

21. There has been no ruling yet determining whether the rule means statute miles per hour or nautical miles per hour.

5 Law in Fog and Restricted Visibility

The rules and regulations for use in restricted visibility are contained in Articles 15 and 16 of the Inland Rules, and Sections 80.12 and 80.13 of the Pilot Rules.

Preliminary

Art. 15 All signals prescribed by this article for vessels underway shall be given:

1. By "steam vessels" on the whistle or siren.
2. By "sailing vessels" and "vessels towed" on the fog horn.

The words "prolonged blast" used in this article shall mean a blast of from four to six seconds' duration.

A steam vessel shall be provided with an efficient whistle or siren, sounded by steam or some substitute for steam, so placed that the sound may not be intercepted by any obstruction, and with an efficient fog horn; also with an efficient bell. A sailing vessel of twenty tons gross tonnage or upward shall be provided with a similar fog horn and bell.

In fog, mist, falling snow, or heavy rain storms, whether by day or night, the signals described in this article shall be used. . . .

The rules in fog should not actually be considered to be limited to "fog, mist, falling snow, or heavy rain storms" as the courts will apply them to restricted visibility due to any cause, as has already happened in a case where visibility was restricted by smoke.[1] Neither the rules nor the courts have provided a distance which defines restricted visibility. Textbook-writers have long recommended the required visibility of sidelights as a guideline, which is presently two miles in the Inland Rules. The courts have required that vessels comply with the rules of fog when near a fog bank, even though they are not themselves experiencing the restricted visibility.[2]

INLAND FOG SIGNALS

The rules prescribe no special signal for a vessel aground in fog. While the courts have ruled that a vessel aground should display the lights and shapes of a vessel at anchor, they have also ruled that the fog signal for a vessel at anchor (rapid ringing of the bell for five seconds) is *not* a proper signal for a vessel aground.[3] A vessel aground may use a distress signal if requiring assistance, or the danger signal to warn other vessels. A vessel aground may also use, if necessary, a "signal to attract attention" from Article 12.

1. The *Gracie*, D.C.N.Y. 1900, 106 F. 984.
2. The *Papoose*, C.C.A.N.Y. 1936, 85 F. 2d 54.
3. The *Leviathan*, N.Y. 1922, 286 F. 745.

The inland fog signals are summarized below. The maximum interval for all inland fog signals is one minute. All vessels in a nest are required to give signals within the statutory interval.

INLAND FOG SIGNALS

KEY: Prolonged blast —
Short blast ·
"Blast," unspecified duration

CATEGORY	SIGNAL	DEVICE
Steam vessel underway	—	Whistle or siren
Steam vessel towing	— · ·	Whistle or siren
Vessel towed	— · ·	Foghorn
Sailing vessel underway		Foghorn
Starboard tack	1 blast	
Port tack	2 blasts	
Wind abaft the beam	3 blasts	
Raft, misc.	1 blast	Foghorn or equivalent
Vessel at anchor*	5-second rapid ringing of bell	
Vessel aground	Danger or distress signal	

*Not required in a "special anchorage area" by:
(1) a vessel of not more than 65 feet in length
(2) a barge, canal boat, scow, or other nondescript craft

Note: Vessels moored at the end of a pier have been required by the courts to "make some noise with a horn, a bell, a gong, or the like."[4]

DANGER SIGNAL IN FOG

The courts have ruled that the danger signal is required in fog when "either vessel fails to understand the course or intention of the other." The one-, two-, and three-short-blast signals are to be given only after vessels have approached to within visual (not radar) sight of each other, at which time the rules for meeting, crossing, or overtaking apply.

MODERATE SPEED

The rules in Article 16 have been strictly applied by the courts:

> Every vessel shall, in a fog, mist, falling snow, or heavy rain storms go at a moderate speed, having careful regard to the existing circumstances and conditions.

A steam vessel hearing, apparently forward of her beam, the fog signal of a vessel the position of which is not ascertained shall, so far as the circumstances of the case admit, stop her engines, and then navigate with caution until danger of collision is over.

Moderate speed has been defined by the courts as follows:

1. Half-distance rule. A vessel should proceed at a speed which enables her to stop in half the distance of the visibility before her.[5] Under some conditions this may mean bare steerageway.

2. If the current and visibility are such that a vessel must go at a speed faster than that required by the half-distance rule in order to maintain bare steerageway, she shall anchor.

3. If the current and visibility are such that a vessel must go at a speed faster than that

---

4. The *Youngstown*, C.C.A.N.Y. 1930, 40 F. 2d 420.

5. *Union Oil of Cal.* v. *Tugboat San Jacinto*, 1972, 93 S. Ct. 368.

required by the half-distance rule in order to maintain bare steerageway, a vessel shall not get underway.

Military vessels exceeding moderate speed due to operational commitments will be found at fault by the courts if the excessive speed contributes to a collision. The owners, the taxpayers of the United States, must pay the damages.

RADAR

Radar is not mentioned in the Inland Rules or Pilot Rules. The courts have made a number of rulings on radar-equipped vessels:

1. Radar is not an excuse for excessive speed.[6]

2. Radar is not an excuse for non-compliance with the Inland Rules.[7] (Lookouts are required, and the engines must be stopped when a fog signal is heard apparently forward of the beam.)

3. Dependable radar equipment must be turned on and intelligent and reasonable use made of it.[8] A manual plot may be required.[9]

4. Vessel rigging her booms in such a way as to greatly impair effective use of her radar is guilty of gross negligence.[10]

5. A fog bank must be searched with radar, and vessel shall reduce speed or stop if necessary until it has been done.[11]

6. The greater the speed at which a vessel is traveling, the greater should be the range setting of her radar.[12]

7. The radar bearing of an approaching vessel which remains fairly constant indicates a collision course and requires immediate, radical avoiding action by the observing vessel.[13]

A district court required the following actions of a radar-equipped vessel:

When the Norscot sighted the Harrison on radar, two miles distant, bearing dead ahead, and the Norscot was proceeding at a speed of 14 knots, she was already in an emergency situation and her engines should have been immediately backed full, her helm put hard right, and her anchors dropped.[14]

SUMMARY OF REQUIREMENTS IN FOG AND RESTRICTED VISIBILITY

1. Display navigation lights.*
2. Proceed at "moderate speed."
3. Sound fog signals.
4. Station lookouts.
5. Make effective use of radar information.**
6. Whenever a fog signal is heard apparently forward of the beam, *stop the engines,* and navigate with caution until clear.

*Not a specific requirement of the rules. A court would probably require it in view of Article 29.
**Not a specific requirement of the rules, but it has been a requirement in court decisions.

6. *Norscot Shipping Co.* v. *S.S. President Harrison*, D.C.Pa. 1970, 308 F. Supp. 1100.

7. *O/Y Finlayson* v. *The Antinous*, D.C.La. 1957, 156 F. Supp. 414.

8. *U.S.* v. *M/V Wuerttemberg*, D.C.S.C. 1963, 219 F. Supp. 211.

9. *Getty Oil Co., Inc.* v. *S.S. Ponce DeLeon*, C.A. N.Y. 1977, 555 F. 2d 328.

10. *Hess Shipping Corp.* v. *S.S. Charles Lykes*, D.C.Ala. 1968, 285 F. Supp. 412.

11. *U.S.* v. *M/V Wuerttemberg.*
12. *Norscot Shipping Co.* v. *S.S. President Harrison.*
13. *Ibid.*
14. *Ibid.*

6 Special Circumstances

The expression *special circumstances* appears in two of the Inland Rules, Articles 27 and 29. According to Article 29, the "Rule of Good Seamanship," special circumstances may require precautions or actions *in addition to* the specific requirements of the other rules. (Good Seamanship is the subject of Chapter 7.) In contrast, Article 27, the "General Prudential Rule," states that special circumstances may require a *departure* from the other rules in order to avoid "immediate danger."

General Prudential Rule

Art. 27 In obeying and construing these rules due regard shall be had to all dangers of navigation and collision, and to any special circumstances which may render a departure from the above rules necessary in order to avoid immediate danger.

In special circumstances, both vessels are burdened and both are required to take action to avoid collision. Special circumstances have been deemed to exist in the following types of situations:

In extremis
Vessel unable to comply with the rules
Approach of a third vessel
Situations not covered by the rules
Departure from the rules by agreement.

IN EXTREMIS

The General Prudential Rule does not imply that the rules do not apply to close quarters situations. The meaning is that in some situations, in the presence of *immediate danger*, obedience to a rule may *cause* a collision.

An "in extremis" situation normally develops when the wrongful actions of a burdened vessel place the privileged vessel in such immediate danger that collision can be avoided only if the privileged vessel departs from the statutory requirement to maintain course and speed. The privileged vessel is *required* by Article 27 to maneuver when in extremis, although the courts have excused masters for not having the presence of mind to choose the best maneuver in the circumstances.

VESSEL UNABLE TO COMPLY WITH THE RULES

It is possible for a vessel to get into a situation where it is not physically possible for her to carry out her obligations under the rules. For example, if a tug with a hawser tow astern would have to back down suddenly in order to avoid a crossing vessel which is privileged, the tug's own tow would very likely collide with her stern. In such a situation, the tug should sound the danger signal to warn the other vessel of her inability to comply with the rules. The privileged vessel is required to stop on hearing the danger signal.

It is possible that the tug may choose to sound two short blasts rather than the danger signal. If the privileged vessel considers this as an unacceptable proposal, she is required to sound the danger signal and stop. The privileged vessel would be justified, due to the special circumstances, in answering the two short blasts with the same signal, and maneuvering to keep out of the way of the tug. Regardless of the signals chosen, the privileged vessel must recognize the apparent conditions and give way. She cannot insist on the right of way in the face of special circumstances.

A towing vessel is not, of course, automatically given the right of way. If a crossing vessel which is privileged can be avoided by slowing down in a timely manner, special circumstances clearly do not exist.

A vessel with a steering or engine casualty

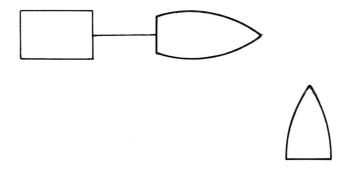

Fig. 34 Special circumstances. Towing vessel unable to keep out of the way.

should similarly sound her inability to abide by the rules with the danger signal. As mentioned in an earlier chapter, there are no lights or shapes for a vessel "not under command" in inland waters to advertise her plight.

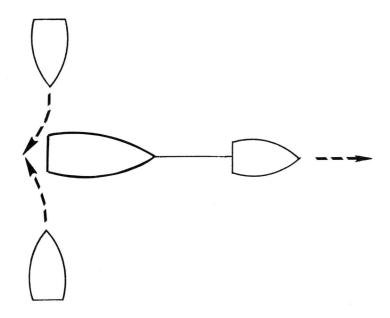

Fig. 35 Special circumstances. Approach of a third vessel.

APPROACH OF A THIRD VESSEL

In some cases more than two vessels may approach each other simultaneously in such a way that signals and maneuvers cannot be handled one at a time. Figure 35 illustrates a case where a schooner was towed out from a pier and ran across a channel between meeting vessels.

In a normal situation both vessels would be required to alter course to starboard when meeting head and head. Both vessels turned to cross under the stern of the schooner and collided. Both vessels were found at fault for failure to recognize the special circumstances and stop.[1] Bridge-to-bridge communications would obviously be of great assistance in situations that involve three or more vessels.

SITUATIONS NOT COVERED BY THE RULES

There are some situations for which the rules provide no specific guidance as to how to maneuver with respect to the other vessel. Examples include "approach situations" where one or both vessels are entering or leaving a slip, maneuvering around piers, or backing. In each case there is a vessel which is not on a steady course. Even though

1. *Shaw* v. *The Reading and the David Smith*, D.C. Pa. 1888, 38 F. 269.

the rules provide signals for a vessel backing or leaving a slip, there are no directions on how to maneuver if an approaching vessel cannot be avoided without one of them taking action. Such situations are "special circumstances" and the rules for meeting, crossing, or overtaking do not apply.

A typical example of how actions in special circumstances would differ from actions required by the other rules would be the case where a vessel on a steady course sights a vessel on her port hand crossing her course while maneuvering around piers. In Figure 36, vessel A would be privileged under the rules for the crossing situation, while the proper action in special circumstances might be to maneuver to the right in order to give the other vessel a wider berth.

Article 27 has also modified the requirement for the privileged vessel. The privileged vessel is legally maintaining course and speed when maneuvering for the following reasons:

1. Stopping her engine and checking her speed preparatory to her landing.[2]
2. Following a channel course that of necessity curves around bends.[3]
3. Stopping to pick up a pilot.[4]

The privileged vessel is required to maneuver in extremis and may maneuver making "such necessary variations in her course as will enable her to avoid immediate danger arising from natural obstructions to navigation."[5]

DEPARTURE FROM THE RULES BY AGREEMENT

There are two situations where departure by agreement can occur. The first is a meeting situation which is meeting "head and head." Vessels who agree to pass starboard to starboard in a head-and-head situation, by the exchange of two-blast signals, place themselves in special circumstances. Vessels similarly place themselves in special circumstances in a crossing situation when the vessels agree, by the exchange of two-blast signals, to the crossing of the privileged vessel's bow.

If a collision results, the vessel proposing the departure is certain to be found at fault, unless the proposal was necessitated by immediate danger. The proposal is not binding on the other vessel, and she may found at fault for the agreement.

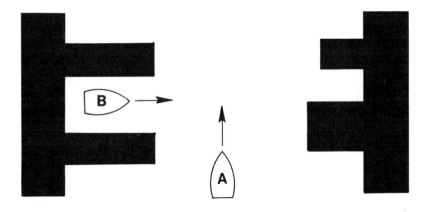

Fig. 36 Special circumstances. Vessel maneuvering around piers.

2. The *D.S.* No. 24, D.C.N.Y. 1943, 52 F. Supp. 648.
3. The *Interstate*, D.C.N.Y. 1922, 280 F. 446.
4. *U.S.* v. *S.S. Soya Atlantic*, C.A. Md. 1964, 330 F. 2d 732.
5. The *John L. Hasbrouck*, 23 L. Ed. 962.

7 Good Seamanship

Article 27 of the Inland Rules discussed special circumstances that may require a *departure* from the other rules. Article 29 "requires in addition to bare compliance with literal provisions of some specific section, adoption either of such additional precautions as it is the ordinary practice of seamen to take in a particular situation, or of such additional precautions as special circumstances of a particular case reasonably demand."[1]

Rule of Good Seamanship

Art. 29 Nothing in these rules shall exonerate any vessel, or the owner or master or crew thereof, from the consequences of any neglect to carry lights or signals, or of any neglect to keep a proper lookout, or of the neglect of any precaution which may be required by the ordinary practice of seamen, or by the special circumstances of the case.

The application of the Rule of Good Seamanship has already become apparent in earlier chapters. Examples include the requirement to sound three short blasts when engines are going less than full speed astern, and the requirements for using radar in Chapter 5. The following list gives other requirements that the courts have found reasonable. Many items listed might lead us to believe that

the Rule of Good Seamanship is politely telling us to use common sense in navigating our vessel.

1. Speed in good visibility
   a. must comply with local regulations
   b. must not create swell or suction which would cause damage to other vessels
   c. must be such that our vessel is completely under control.
2. Vessels must not pass unnecessarily near to pier ends.
3. Vessels must be properly manned and steered.
4. Vessels must not navigate with defective equipment.
5. A vessel has the "responsibility to utilize available weather reports so that it can operate in manner consistent with foreseeable risk."[2]
6. Vessels moored must have sufficient mooring lines.
7. Anchored vessels must have sufficient chain out, and drop a second anchor if the circumstances require it.
8. "A navigator is chargeable with knowledge

1. *U.S.* v. *Woodbury*, C.A. Mass. 1949, 175 F. 2d 854.

2. *M.P. Howlett Inc.* v. *Tug Dalzellido*, D.C.N.Y. 1971, 324 F. Supp. 912.

of the maneuvering capacity of his vessel. He is bound to know the character of his vessel and how she would turn in ordinary conditions."[3]

9. "When a vessel is known to be about to enter or leave a dock, other vessels should keep well clear and avoid embarrassing her maneuvers."[4]

10. "In waters well frequented by small tows . . . the law requires that a ship should have a competent person standing by in the forecastle ready at a moment's notice to let go the anchors."[5]

11. "Where two steamers about to meet are running one with and the other against the tide, if it be necessary that one or the other should stop in order to avoid a collision, the one proceeding against the tide should stop."[6]

12. Special circumstances may require that an anchor watch be maintained.

13. Vessels must not anchor too close to other vessels already at anchor.

The courts have also given legal meaning to the term *proper lookout.*

1. "Lookout is person who is specially charged with duty of observing lights, sounds, echoes, or any obstruction to navigation."[7]

2. "Lookouts, who must be kept on all vessels, must be persons of suitable experience, properly stationed on vessel, and actually and vigilantly employed in the performance of that duty."[8]

3. "Lookout should be placed as low and as far forward as possible."[9] This is a requirement in clear weather as well as in fog if failure to comply can result in any one of the following:
   a. the lookout does not have a clear, unobstructed view
   b. the lookout's ability to hear signals is impaired
   c. the lookout will sight a danger earlier if placed forward (as when leaving a blind slip).

4. "Lookout . . . should have no other duties."[10]

5. The circumstances will dictate the number of lookouts required. The number must be sufficient to detect any reasonably foreseen danger from any direction.

6. A lookout astern is required when backing.

7. Lookouts must have a direct and positive means of communicating what they observe to the conning officer. "If the lookout cannot, or does not, report his observations, improper watch is being maintained."[11] A lookout cannot wear headphones, as his ability to hear signals would be impaired.

3. *City of New York* v. *Morania No. 12 Inc.,* 1973, 357 F. Supp. 234.
4. *Ibid.*
5. *River Terminals Corp.* v. *U.S.,* D.C. La. 1954, 121 F. Supp. 98.
6. The *Galatea,* N.Y. 1876, 23 L. Ed. 727.
7. *Sun Oil Co.* v. *S.S. Georgel,* D.C.N.Y. 1969, 245 F. Supp. 537.
8. *Jett* v. *Texas Co.,* D.C. Del. 1947, 73 F. Supp. 699.
9. The *Kaga Maru,* D.C. Wash. 1927, 18 F. 2d 295.
10. *U.S.* v. *The Holland,* D.C. Md. 1957, 151 F. Supp. 772.
11. *U.S.* v. *Tug Collette Malloy,* C.C.A. Tex. 1975, 507 F. 2d 1019.

PART 2
International Waters

1 Introduction to the International Rules

The 1972 Rules Conference which produced the most recent revision of the International Rules marked the conclusion of four years of effort by national committees and international working groups. One of the foremost desires of those groups was that the rules be simplified and aimed at the mariner, not at those who practice admiralty law. The intent of the rules is to provide the mariner with a practical code for safely maneuvering his ship with relation to others.

A notable feature of the rules is the absence of terms which will require extensive legal definitions by the courts. As an example, the rules require that vessels proceed at a safe speed at all times. The rules do not stop there, but go on to give a comprehensive list of factors which must be taken into account in order to determine a safe speed appropriate to the prevailing circumstances and conditions.

The rules are organized in the following manner:

Part A — General

Part B — Steering and Sailing Rules
Section I — Conduct of Vessels in Any Condition of Visibility
Section II — Conduct of Vessels in Sight of One Another
Section III — Conduct of Vessels in Restricted Visibility
Part C — Lights and Shapes
Part D — Sound and Light Signals
Part E — Exemptions
Annex I — Positioning and Technical Details of Lights and Shapes
Annex II — Additional Signals for Fishing Vessels Fishing in Close Proximity
Annex III — Technical Details of Sound Signal Appliances
Annex IV — Distress Signals

Of special significance is the organization of Part B — Steering and Sailing Rules. Note, for instance, that vessels in fog are governed by Section I as well as by Section III.

DEFINITIONS

Rule 3 — General Definitions

For the purpose of these rules, except where the context otherwise requires:

(a) The word "vessel" includes every description of water craft, including nondisplacement craft and seaplanes, used or capable of being used as a means of transportation on water.

(b) The term "power-driven vessel" means any vessel propelled by machinery.

(c) The term "sailing vessel" means any vessel under sail provided that propelling machinery, if fitted, is not being used.

(d) The term "vessel engaged in fishing" means any vessel fishing with nets, lines, trawls or other fishing apparatus which restrict manoeuvrability, but does not include a vessel fishing with trolling lines or other fishing apparatus which do not restrict manoeuvrability.

(e) The word "seaplane" includes any aircraft designed to manoeuvre on the water.

(f) The term "vessel not under command" means a vessel which through some exceptional circumstance is unable to manoeuvre as required by these rules and is therefore unable to keep out of the way of another vessel.

(g) The term "vessel restricted in her ability to manoeuvre" means a vessel which from the nature of her work is restricted in her ability to manoeuvre as required by these rules and is therefore unable to keep out of the way of another vessel.

The following vessels shall be regarded as vessels restricted in their ability to manoeuvre:

(i) a vessel engaged in laying, servicing or picking up a navigation mark, submarine cable or pipeline;

(ii) a vessel engaged in dredging, surveying or underwater operations;

(iii) a vessel engaged in replenishment or transferring persons, provisions or cargo while underway;

(iv) a vessel engaged in the launching or recovery of aircraft;

(v) a vessel engaged in minesweeping operations;

(vi) a vessel engaged in a towing operation such as severely restricts the towing vessel and her tow in their ability to deviate from their course.

(h) The term "vessel constrained by her draught" means a power-driven vessel which because of her draught in relation to the available depth of water is severely restricted in her ability to deviate from the course she is following:

(i) The word "underway" means that a vessel is not at anchor, or made fast to the shore, or aground.

(j) The words "length" and "breadth" of a vessel mean her length overall and greatest breadth.

(k) Vessels shall be deemed to be in sight of one another only when one can be observed visually from the other.

(l) The term "restricted visibility" means any condition in which visibility is restricted by fog, mist, falling snow, heavy rainstorms, sandstorms or any other similar causes.

Rule 32 — Definitions [from Part D]

(a) The word "whistle" means any sound signalling appliance capable of producing the prescribed blasts and which complies with the specifications in Annex III to these regulations.

(b) The term "short blast" means a blast of about one second's duration.

(c) The term "prolonged blast" means a blast of from four to six seconds' duration.

2 Lights and Shapes

The basic purpose of lights is to warn vessels of the presence or approach of other vessels, and to aid in determining the course and aspect of vessels underway. The International Rules contain a comprehensive hierarchy for "responsibilities between vessels" (right of way). By observing the lights or shapes displayed by an approaching vessel, the mariner can determine which vessel has the responsibility to keep out of the way of the other.

The International Rules for lights and shapes are found in Part C.

Rule 20 — Application

(a) Rules in this part shall be complied with in all weathers.

(b) The rules concerning lights shall be complied with from sunset to sunrise, and during such times no other lights shall be exhibited, except such lights as cannot be mistaken for the lights specified in these rules or do not impair their visibility or distinctive character, or interfere with the keeping of a proper look-out.

(c) The lights prescribed by these rules shall, if carried, also be exhibited from sunrise to sunset in restricted visibility and may be exhibited in all other circumstances when it is deemed necessary.

(d) The rules concerning shapes shall be complied with by day.

(e) The lights and shapes specified in these rules shall comply with the provisions of Annex I to these regulations.

Note that lights are *required* to be shown in restricted visibility as well as at night. Lights may also be shown at any other time when deemed necessary.

Certain vessels are required to show additional lights "when making way through the water." *Making way* refers to motion caused by the engines or propelling machinery, not to motion caused by drifting with the current. A vessel which is not at anchor, or made fast to the shore, or aground, while dead in the water, is considered a vessel "underway but stopped and making no way through the water."

TERMS

The following terms will be used in this text to describe the lights and shapes prescribed by the International Rules. Note that *all the shapes are black.*

Masthead light   A 20-point white light at the forward masthead, showing an arc from dead ahead to 2 points (22.5 degrees) abaft the beam on both sides.

Range light   A 20-point white light abaft of and higher than the masthead light. It is in line with the masthead light (forms a range) if the vessel is seen from dead ahead. In every case where the range light is required for a vessel 50 meters and upward in length, it is optional for a vessel less than 50 meters in length. For the sake of brevity, the above details will be omitted from the diagrams on the following pages, and an asterisk (*) shown as a reminder.

Sternlight   A 12-point white light showing 6 points from right aft on each side.

Sidelights   A red light on the port side, and a green light on the starboard side. Both are 10-point lights showing from dead ahead to 2 points (22.5 degrees) abaft the beam on their respective sides.

Towing masthead lights   Two or three lights of the same character as the 20-point masthead light.

Yellow towing light   A 12-point yellow light, showing over the same arc as would a 12-point sternlight.

Diamond shape   A shape consisting of two cones having a common base.

POWER-DRIVEN VESSELS

Figure 37

Required lights

Masthead light (20-point)

Range light   (20-point)

Sidelights   (10-point)

Sternlight   (12-point)

An air-cushion vessel operating in the non-displacement mode is required to show a flashing yellow light (32-point) in addition to the above lights.

Note

When a pushing vessel and a vessel being pushed are rigidly connected in a composite unit, they shall be regarded as a power-driven vessel and show the above lights.

Figure 38

Required lights

Masthead light (20-point)

Sidelights   (10-point)

Sternlight   (12-point)

An air-cushion vessel operating in the non-displacement mode is required to show a flashing yellow light (32-point) in addition to the above lights.

Other lights

20-point range light is optional (not shown in Figure 38)

Note

Same as above.

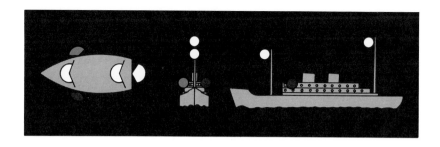

Fig. 37 Power-driven vessel — 50 meters and upward in length. International Rule 23.

Fig. 38 Power-driven vessel — less than 50 meters in length. International Rule 23.

Fig. 39 Power-driven vessel less than 50 meters in length towing astern. Length of tow does not exceed 200 meters. International Rule 24.

Fig. 40 Power-driven vessel less than 50 meters in length towing astern. Length of tow greater than 200 meters. International Rule 24.

Fig. 41 Power-driven vessel 50 meters and upward in length towing astern. Length of tow does not exceed 200 meters. International Rule 24.

VESSELS ENGAGED IN TOWING

Figure 39

Required lights

    2 towing masthead lights (20-point)
    Sidelights   (10-point)
    Sternlight   (12-point)
    Yellow towing light   (12-point)

Other lights

    20-point range light is optional (not shown in Figure 39)

Figure 40

Required lights

    3 towing masthead lights (20-point)
    Sidelights   (10-point)
    Sternlight   (12-point)
    Yellow towing light   (12-point)

Other lights

    20-point range light is optional (not shown in Figure 40)

Dayshape

    Diamond where best seen

Figure 41

Required lights

    2 towing masthead lights (20-point)
    Range light   (20-point)
    Sidelights   (10-point)
    Sternlight   (12-point)
    Yellow towing light   (12-point)

Vessels Engaged in Towing (cont.)

Figure 42

Required lights

3 towing masthead lights (20-point)
Range light   (20-point)
Sidelights   (10-point)
Sternlight   (12-point)
Yellow towing light   (12-point)

Dayshape

Diamond where best seen

Fig. 42 Power-driven vessel 50 meters and upward in length towing astern. Length of tow greater than 200 meters. International Rule 24.

Figure 43

Required lights

2 towing masthead lights
Red–white–red (32-point) in a vertical line where best seen
*Range light (20-point) — not shown in Figure 43 (*see* page 64)
Sidelights (10-point)
Sternlight (12-point)
Yellow towing light (12-point)

Dayshapes

Ball–diamond–ball in vertical line where best seen

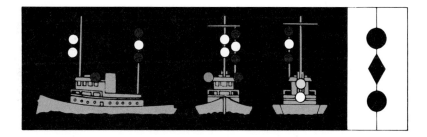

Fig. 43 Vessel towing — severely restricted in ability to deviate from course. Length of tow does not exceed 200 meters. International Rule 27.

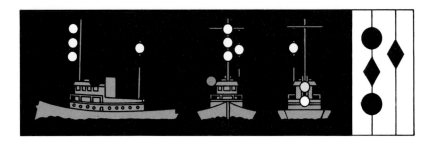

Fig. 44 Vessel towing — severely restricted in ability to deviate from course. Length of tow greater than 200 meters. International Rule 27.

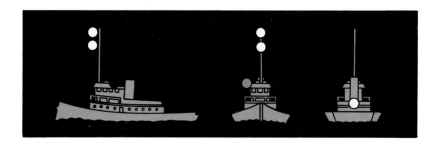

Fig. 45 Power-driven vessel pushing ahead or towing alongside. International Rule 24.

Vessels Engaged in Towing (cont.)

Figure 44

Required lights

> 3 towing masthead lights
> Red–white–red (32-point) in a vertical line where best seen
> *Range light (20-point) — not shown in Figure 44 (*see* page 64)
> Sidelights (10-point)
> Sternlight (12-point)
> Yellow towing light (12-point)

Dayshapes

> Ball–diamond–ball in vertical line where best seen
> Diamond where best seen

Figure 45

Required lights

> 2 masthead towing lights (20-point)
> *Range light (20-point) — not shown in Figure 45 (*see* page 64)
> Sidelights (10-point)
> Sternlight (12-point)

Note

> When a pushing vessel and a vessel being pushed ahead are rigidly connected in a composite unit they shall be regarded as a power-driven vessel and exhibit the lights prescribed in Rule 23.

VESSELS IN TOW

Figure 46

Required lights

Sidelights (10-point) at forward end

Notes

Any number of vessels being towed or pushed in a group shall be lighted as one vessel.

When a pushing vessel and a vessel being pushed ahead are rigidly connected in a composite unit they shall be regarded as a power-driven vessel and exhibit the lights prescribed in Rule 23.

Fig. 46 Vessel being pushed ahead. International Rule 24.

Figure 47

Required lights

Sidelights (10-point)

Sternlight (12-point)

Dayshape

Diamond where best seen, when length of tow exceeds 200 meters

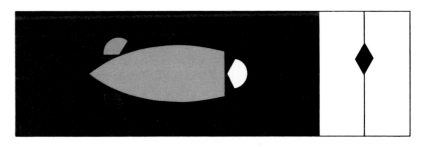

Fig. 47 Vessel being towed astern. International Rule 24.

Figure 48

Required lights

Sidelights at forward end   (10-point)

Sternlight   (12-point)

Fig. 48 Vessel being towed alongside. International Rule 24.

Fig. 49 Sailing vessel underway. International Rule 25.

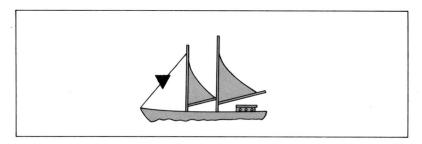

Fig. 50 Vessel proceeding under sail when also being propelled by machinery. International Rule 25.

Fig. 51 Vessel engaged in trawling — left, not making way; center, making way. International Rule 26.

SAILING VESSELS

Figures 49 and 50

Required lights

Sidelights (10-point)

Sternlight (12-point)

Other lights

Red over green (32-point) at or near the top of the mast, optional

Note

Sailing vessel less than 12 meters in length may combine sidelights and sternlight in one lantern placed at or near the top of the mast. The optional red over green lights may not be shown with such a lantern.

Dayshape

Conical shape, apex down, where best seen

FISHING VESSELS

Figure 51

Required lights

Green over white at masthead (32-point)

*Range light (20-point) higher than green light when displayed — not shown in Figure 51 (*see* page 64)

Sidelights and sternlight required *only when making way through the water.*

Dayshapes

2 cones with apexes together in a vertical line. A vessel of less than 20 meters in length may substitute a basket for these shapes.

Vessels Engaged in Fishing (cont.)

Figure 52

Required lights

Red over white at masthead (32-point)

White light (32-point) required if outlying gear extends more than 150 meters horizontally from vessel. Must be placed to show direction toward the gear (not shown in Figure 52)

Sidelights and sternlight required *only when making way through the water.*

Dayshapes

2 cones with apexes together in a vertical line. A vessel less than 20 meters may substitute a basket for these shapes.

Cone apex upward to show direction of outlying gear if gear extends more than 150 meters horizontally from the vessel.

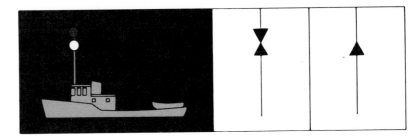

Fig. 52 Vessel engaged in fishing (underway or at anchor). International Rule 26.

VESSELS NOT UNDER COMMAND

Figure 53

Required lights

Red over red (32-point) in vertical line where best seen

Sidelights and sternlight *only if making way through the water*

Dayshapes

2 balls in a vertical line where best seen

Fig. 53 Vessel not under command — left, not making way; right, making way. International Rule 27.

Fig. 54 Vessel restricted in her ability to maneuver (special operations), except vessel engaged in minesweeping — left, not making way; right, making way. International Rule 27.

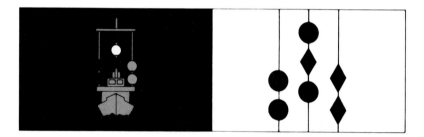

Fig. 55 Vessel engaged in dredging or underway operations, when restricted in her ability to maneuver. International Rule 27.

VESSELS RESTRICTED IN THEIR ABILITY TO MANEUVER

Figure 54

Required lights

Red–white–red (32-point) in a vertical line where best seen

Masthead, *range light (*see* page 64), sidelights and sternlight shown *only if making way through the water*

Dayshapes

Ball–diamond–ball in a vertical line where best seen

Note

When at anchor, red–white–red lights shown *in addition to* anchor lights.

Figure 55

Required lights

Red–white–red (32-point) in a vertical line where best seen

When an obstruction exists:

obstructed side — red over red (32-point)

clear side — green over green (32-point)

Masthead light, *range light (*see* page 64), sidelights and sternlight shown *only when making way through the water* (not shown in Figure 55)

Dayshapes

2 balls in a vertical line on obstructed side

Ball–diamond–ball in a vertical line where best seen

2 diamonds in a vertical line on clear side

Note

The lights and shapes shown in the diagram are required when underway with no way on. They are also the only lights and shapes required to be shown when at anchor.

Vessels Restricted in Their Ability to Maneuver (cont.)

Figure 56

Dayshape

Rigid replica of the International Code flag "Alpha"

VESSELS ENGAGED IN MINESWEEPING

Figure 57

Required lights

3 green lights (32-point), one at foremast head and one at each end of fore yard

Masthead light (20-point)

*Range light (20-point) — not shown in Figure 57 (*see* page 64)

Sidelights (10-point)

Sternlight (12-point)

Dayshapes

3 balls in same position as the green lights

Note

These lights and shapes indicate that it is dangerous to approach closer than 1,000 meters astern or 500 meters on either side.

VESSELS CONSTRAINED BY DRAFT

Figure 58

Required lights

Normal lights for a power-driven vessel

Other lights

3 red lights (32-point) in a vertical line where best seen, optional

Dayshape

Cylinder where best seen, optional

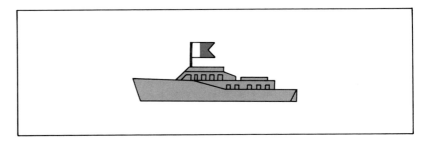

Fig. 56 Diving operations — when size of vessel makes it impractical to exhibit the shapes shown above. International Rule 27.

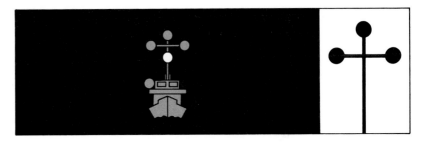

Fig. 57 Vessel engaged in minesweeping. International Rule 27.

Fig. 58 Vessel constrained by draft. International Rule 28.

Fig. 59 Pilot vessel underway. International Rule 29.

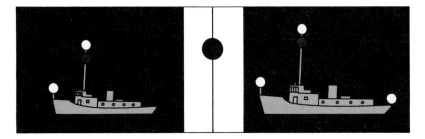

Fig. 60 Pilot vessel at anchor — left, less than 50 meters in length; right, 50 meters and upward. International Rule 29.

Fig. 61 Vessel at anchor. International Rule 30.

PILOT VESSELS

Figure 59

Required lights

White over red (32-point) in a vertical line at or near the masthead
Sidelights (10-point)
Sternlight (12-point)

Figure 60

Required lights

White over red (32-point) in a vertical line at or near the masthead
Anchor lights for a vessel of her length

Dayshape

One ball

VESSELS AT ANCHOR

Figure 61

Required lights

White light (32-point) in fore part of vessel
White light (32-point) near the stern and lower than the forward light

Other lights

A vessel of less than 50 meters in length may substitute one white light (32-point) where best seen

Dayshape

One ball where best seen

Note

Vessels of 100 meters and more in length are required to illuminate their decks, optional for smaller vessels.

VESSELS AGROUND

Figure 62

Required lights

Red over red (32-point) in a vertical line where best seen

Anchor lights for a vessel of her length

Dayshapes

3 balls in a vertical line where best seen

SUMMARY OF IMPORTANT PROVISIONS

A *power-driven vessel* of any length, when underway, is required to show a masthead light, sidelights and sternlight. The after range light is required for vessels of 50 meters and upward in length, and optional for smaller vessels.

A *power-driven vessel engaged in towing or pushing* displays two towing masthead lights, except when towing astern and the length of the tow exceeds 200 meters, in which case she shows three towing masthead lights. A yellow towing light is displayed above the sternlight only when towing astern. A vessel "engaged in a towing operation such as severely restricts the towing vessel and her tow in their ability to deviate from their course" shows the red–white–red lights in a vertical line *in addition to* the other lights displayed by a towing vessel; she also shows the ball–diamond–ball shapes in the daytime. If towing astern and the length of the tow exceeds 200 meters, a diamond is displayed by both the towing vessel and the tow.

Vessels *engaged in fishing or trawling*, and vessels *not under command* display sidelights and a sternlight only when making way through the water. The special arrays all include two 32-point lights: red over white for fishing; green over white

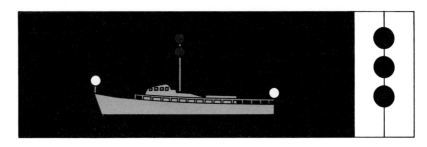

Fig. 62 Vessel aground. International Rule 30.

for trawling; and red over red for not under command. Other lights include: the white light for a vessel engaged in fishing with gear extending more than 150 meters horizontally from the vessel; and the after range light for the trawler (optional if length of trawler is less than 50 meters).

Vessels restricted in their ability to maneuver, except minesweepers and towing vessels, display a masthead light, range light, sidelights and sternlight only if making way through the water. The special array is the red–white–red lights in a vertical line. A vessel engaged in dredging or underwater operations also shows the two red lights on the obstructed side, and two green lights on the clear side.

A *vessel engaged in minesweeping* shows three green lights or three balls in addition to the lights for a power-driven vessel.

A *vessel constrained by her draft* is permitted to show three red lights in a vertical line or a cylinder in addition to the lights for a power-driven vessel.

All *pilot vessels* underway and engaged in pilotage duty show white over red 32-point lights in addition to sidelights and a sternlight.

Vessels at anchor are required to show two white 32-point lights, with the forward light the higher of the two. A vessel less than 50 meters in length may instead show only one light. A vessel restricted in her ability to maneuver, except minesweepers and towing vessels, shows the anchor light(s) or shape *in addition to* the red–white–red lights or ball–diamond–ball shapes. A pilot vessel shows the white over red lights in addition to the anchor light(s). A vessel engaged in dredging or underwater operations while at anchor shows *only* the red–white–red lights, the two green lights and

the two red lights, or the corresponding shapes in the daytime. A fishing vessel does not show anchor lights, being required to show the same lights at anchor that she shows when underway with no way on.

A *vessel aground* shows two 32-point lights, red over red, in addition to her anchor light(s), or three balls during the day.

A *vessel proceeding under sail and power* is required to show a cone, point down. A vessel displaying this shape is a "power-driven vessel" for the purpose of the other rules.

Sailing vessels underway have the option of showing red over green (32-point) lights at the masthead in addition to the required sidelights and sternlight.

MISCELLANEOUS INTERNATIONAL PROVISIONS

Rule 37 — Distress Signals

When a vessel is in distress and requires assistance she shall use or exhibit the signals prescribed in Annex IV to these regulations.

Annex IV — Distress Signals

1. The following signals, used or exhibited either together or separately, indicate distress and need of assistance:

(a) a gun or other explosive signal fired at intervals of about a minute;

(b) a continuous sounding with any fog-signalling apparatus;

(c) rockets or shells, throwing red stars fired one at a time at short intervals;

(d) a signal made by radiotelegraphy or by any other signalling method consisting of the group · · · — — — · · · (SOS) in the Morse Code;

(e) a signal sent by radiotelephony consisting of the spoken word "Mayday";

(f) the International Code Signal of distress indicated by N.C.;

(g) a signal consisting of a square flag having above or below it a ball or anything resembling a ball;

(h) flames on the vessel (as from a burning tar barrel, oil barrel, etc.)

(i) a rocket parachute flare or a hand flare showing a red light;

(j) a smoke signal giving off orange-coloured smoke;

(k) slowly and repeatedly raising and lowering arms outstretched to each side;

(l) the radiotelegraph alarm signal;

(m) the radiotelephone alarm signal;

(n) signals transmitted by emergency position-indicating radio beacons.

2. The use or exhibition of any of the foregoing signals except for the purpose of indicating distress and need of assistance and the use of other signals which may be confused with any of the above signals is prohibited.

3. Attention is drawn to the relevant sections of the International Code of Signals, the Merchant Ship Search and Rescue Manual and the following signals:

(a) a piece of orange-coloured canvas with either a black square and circle or other appropriate symbol (for identification from the air);

(b) a dye marker.

Note: Although not specified in the rules, a distress signal that is accepted by custom is an inverted ensign, both in inland and international waters. However, such a signal is not appropriate for use by a man-of-war.

Rule 36 — Signals to Attract Attention

If necessary to attract the attention of another vessel, any vessel may make light or sound signals that cannot be mistaken for any signal authorized elsewhere in these rules, or may direct the beam of her searchlight in the direction of the danger, in such a way as not to embarrass any vessel.

Rule 1(c) — Additional Station Lights, Signal Lights, or Whistle Signals

Nothing in these rules shall interfere with the operation of any special rules made by the Government of any State with respect to additional station or signal lights or whistle signals for ships of war and vessels proceeding under convoy, or with respect to additional station or signal lights for fishing vessels engaged in fishing as a fleet. These additional station or signal lights or whistle signals shall, so far as possible, be such that they cannot be mistaken for any light or signal authorized elsewhere under these rules.

Rule 1(e) — Vessels of Special Construction or Purpose

Whenever the Government concerned shall have determined that a vessel of special construction or purpose cannot comply fully with the provisions of any of these rules with respect to the number, position, range or arc of visibility of lights or shapes, as well as to the disposition and characteristics of sound-signalling appliances, without interfering with the special function of the vessel, such vessel shall comply with such other provisions in regard to the number, position, range or arc of visibility of lights or shapes, as well as to the disposition and characteristics of sound-signalling appliances, as her Government shall have determined to be the closest possible compliance with these rules in respect to that vessel.

Under this authority, the United States has passed laws authorizing the Secretary of the Navy and the Secretary of Transportation to exempt Navy and Coast Guard vessels of special construction from certain requirements pertaining to lights.[1] The Coast Guard exceptions are published in Title 33, Code of Federal Regulations, Part 135. Light waivers for naval vessels are published in Title 32, Code of Federal Regulations, Part 706. Such exceptions are reproduced in CG-169.

Submarines

U.S. naval submarines are required to display an intermittent flashing (yellow) beacon with a sequential operation of one flash per second for 3 seconds, followed by a 3-second off period. The light will be exhibited in addition to the other navigational lights for submarines, and displayed in both inland and international waters. (Part 707 of Title 32, Code of Federal Regulations.)

Reduced Lighting Requirements for Small Vessels

Several of the rules permit reduced lighting requirements for small vessels. These provisions were not included in the preceding diagrams.

A *power-driven vessel* of less than 7 meters in length and whose maximum speed does not exceed 7 knots may show one 32-point light in lieu of all other lights, but such a vessel shall, if practicable, also exhibit sidelights (Rule 23).

A *sailing vessel* of less than 7 meters in length shall, if practicable, exhibit sidelights and a sternlight, or a single lantern at or near the top of the mast combining sidelights and a sternlight. If she does not, she shall have at hand a white light which shall be exhibited in sufficient time to prevent collision (Rule 25).

A *vessel under oars* may exhibit sidelights and a sternlight, but if she does not, she shall have at hand a white light which shall be exhibited in sufficient time to prevent collision (Rule 25).

Vessels less than 7 meters in length are not required to show the lights of Rule 27 for *vessels not under command or restricted in their ability to maneuver.*

A vessel of less than 7 meters in length, when *at anchor or aground*, not in or near a narrow channel, fairway or anchorage, or where other vessels normally navigate, is not required to exhibit anchor lights or shapes (Rule 30).

---

1. 33 USC 1052 and 33 USC 360.

3 Responsibilities Between Vessels — Right of Way

This chapter discusses the International Rules concerning the right of way between different categories of vessels underway, namely:

CATEGORY	SPECIAL LIGHT ARRAY
Not under command	Red over red
Restricted in ability to maneuver	Red–white–red
Minesweeper	3 green lights
Constrained by draft	Red–red–red
Engaged in fishing	Red over white
Engaged in trawling	Green over white
Sailing vessel	Red over green (optional)
Power-driven vessel	None
Includes: Pilot vessel	White over red
Towing vessel	Towing masthead lights

All vessels underway must keep out of the way of vessels at anchor or aground.

BURDENED AND PRIVILEGED DUTIES

Rule 16 — Action by Give-Way Vessel

Every vessel which is directed to keep out of the way of another vessel shall, so far as possible, take early and substantial action to keep well clear.

Action to Avoid Collision (excerpt from Rule 8)

Any action taken to avoid collision shall, if the circumstances of the case admit, be positive, made in ample time and with due regard to the observance of good seamanship.

Any alteration of course and/or speed to avoid collision shall, if the circumstances of the case admit, be large enough to be readily apparent to another vessel observing visually or by radar; a succession of small alterations of course and/or speed should be avoided.

If there is sufficient sea room, alteration of course alone may be the most effective action to avoid a close-quarters situation provided that it is made in good time, is substantial and does not result in another close-quarters situation.

Action taken to avoid collision with another vessel shall be such as to result in passing at a safe distance. The effectiveness of the action shall be carefully checked until the other vessel is finally past and clear.

Action by Stand-On Vessel (excerpt from Rule 17)

Where one of two vessels is to keep out of the way, the other shall keep her course and speed.

The latter vessel may however take action to avoid collision by her manoeuvre alone, as soon as it becomes apparent to her that the vessel required to keep out of the way is not taking appropriate action in compliance with these rules.

When, from any cause, the vessel required to keep her course and speed finds herself so close that collision cannot be avoided by the action of the give-way vessel alone, she shall take such action as will best aid to avoid collision.

This rule does not relieve the give-way vessel of her obligation to keep out of the way.

Right of Way Between Different Categories of Vessels

Rule 18 provides a hierarchy of "responsibilities between vessels." Except where Rule 9 (Narrow Channels), Rule 10 (Traffic Separation Schemes) or Rule 13 (Overtaking) otherwise require, all vessels underway shall keep out of the way of vessels in all categories which are listed above the category pertaining to their own vessel:

1. A vessel not under command/a vessel restricted in her ability to maneuver (including a vessel engaged in minesweeping operations).
2. A vessel constrained by her draft.
3. A vessel engaged in fishing.
4. A sailing vessel.
5. A power-driven vessel.

Narrow Channels (excerpt from Rule 9)

A vessel of less than 20 meters in length or a sailing vessel shall not impede the passage of a vessel which can safely navigate only within a narrow channel or fairway.

A vessel engaged in fishing shall not impede the passage of any other vessel navigating within a narrow channel or fairway.

A vessel shall not cross a narrow channel or fairway if such crossing impedes the passage of a vessel which can safely navigate only within such channel or fairway. The latter vessel may use the sound signal prescribed in Rule 34(d) [international signal of doubt, 5 or more short blasts], if in doubt as to the intention of the crossing vessel.

Traffic-Separation Schemes (excerpt from Rule 10)

A vessel of less than 20 meters in length or a sailing vessel shall not impede the safe passage of a power-driven vessel following a traffic lane.

A vessel engaged in fishing shall not impede the passage of any vessel following a traffic lane.

A vessel not using a traffic separation scheme shall avoid it by as wide a margin as is practicable.

A vessel shall so far as practicable avoid crossing traffic lanes, but if obliged to do so shall cross as nearly as practicable at right angles to the general direction of traffic flow.

Overtaking (excerpt from Rule 13)

Any vessel overtaking any other shall keep out of the way of the vessel being overtaken.

RIGHT OF WAY — SAILING VESSEL APPROACHING SAILING VESSEL

Rule 12 — Sailing Vessels
(a) When two sailing vessels are approaching one another, so as to involve risk of collision, one

of them shall keep out of the way of the other as follows:

    (i) When each has the wind on a different side, the vessel which has the wind on the port side shall keep out of the way of the other.

    (ii) When both have the wind on the same side, the vessel which is to windward shall keep out of the way of the vessel which is to leeward.

    (iii) If a vessel with the wind on the port side sees a vessel to windward and cannot determine with certainty whether the other vessel has the wind on the port or on the starboard side, she shall keep out of the way of the other.

(b) For the purposes of this rule the windward side shall be deemed to be the side opposite to that on which the mainsail is carried or, in the case of a square-rigged vessel, the side opposite to that on which the largest fore-and-aft sail is carried.

4 Approach Situations Between Power-Driven Vessels in Sight

Chapter 3 was concerned with the right of way between different categories of vessels as well as the right of way between two sailing vessels. The privileged or burdened status of two power-driven vessels approaching each other on the high seas is determined by the approach situation — overtaking, meeting, or crossing. Two conditions are necessary before any of the three approach situations can exist between two power-driven vessels:

1. There must be a risk of collision.
2. The two power-driven vessels must be in sight of each other.

Risk of collision shall be deemed to exist if the compass bearing (not relative bearing) of an approaching vessel does not appreciably change. If there is any doubt, assume that there is a risk of collision.

The meeting, overtaking, and crossing situations apply only to vessels in sight, which does not include tracking by radar. The situations apply in fog and other conditions of restricted visibility, *but only after the vessels have sighted each other*.

MANEUVERING SIGNALS (excerpt from Rule 34)

(a) When vessels are in sight of one another, a power-driven vessel underway, when manoeuvering as authorized or required by these rules, shall indicate that manoeuvre by the following signals on her whistle:

—one short blast to mean "I am altering my course to starboard";
—two short blasts to mean "I am altering my course to port";
—three short blasts to mean "I am operating astern propulsion."

(b) Any vessel may supplement the whistle signals prescribed in paragraph (a) of this rule by light signals, repeated as appropriate, whilst the manoeuvre is being carried out.

(i) these light signals shall have the following significance:

—one flash to mean "I am altering my course to starboard";

—two flashes to mean "I am altering my course to port";

—three flashes to mean "I am operating astern propulsion";

(ii) the duration of each flash shall be about one second, the interval between flashes shall be about one second, and the interval between successive signals shall be not less than ten seconds;

(iii) the light used for this signal shall, if fitted, be an all-round white light, visible at a minimum range of 5 miles, and shall comply with the provisions of Annex I.

The one- and two-short-blast signals are required to be given only by power-driven vessels, when a vessel of any type or category is in sight. They are rudder-action signals, intended to inform other vessels that a change of course is being executed. The signal requires no answer from other vessels.

The backing signal of three short blasts is required to be given only by power-driven vessels, when a vessel of any type or category is in sight.

The light signals which can supplement the one-, two-, or three-short-blast signals are optional.

INTERNATIONAL SIGNAL OF DOUBT — DANGER SIGNAL (Rule 34(d))

When vessels in sight of one another are approaching each other and from any cause either vessel fails to understand the intentions or actions of the other, or is in doubt whether sufficient action is being taken by the other to avoid collision, the vessel in doubt shall immediately indicate such doubt by giving at least five short and rapid blasts on the whistle. Such signal may be supplemented by a light signal of at least five short and rapid flashes.

Note that this rule does not confine the use of the doubt signal to power-driven vessels, but requires it to be given by "every description of water craft, including nondisplacement craft and seaplanes, used or capable of being used as a means of transportation on the water." Rule 33 requires a vessel of 12 meters or more in length to have a whistle complying with the specifications in Annex III, and requires smaller vessels to "be provided with some other means of making an efficient sound signal." The doubt or danger signal, like the rudder and backing signals, is given only when vessels are in sight of one another. The signal is required by the vessel in doubt, which may be *either* a burdened or a privileged vessel.

OVERTAKING SITUATIONS

Rule 13 — Overtaking

(a) Notwithstanding anything contained in the rules of this Section any vessel overtaking any other shall keep out of the way of the vessel being overtaken.

(b) A vessel shall be deemed to be overtaking when coming up with another vessel from a direction more than 22.5 degrees abaft her beam, that is, in such a position with reference to the vessel she is overtaking, that at night she would be able to see only the sternlight of that vessel but neither of her sidelights.

(c) When a vessel is in any doubt as to whether

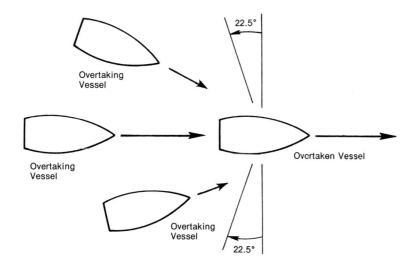

Fig. 63 Overtaking situation.

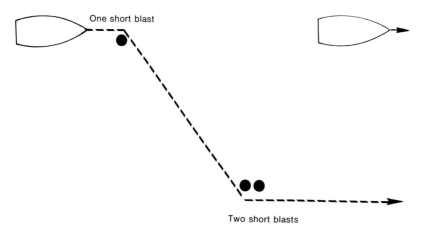

Fig. 64 Overtaking in open waters.

she is overtaking another, she shall assume that this is the case and act accordingly.

(d) Any subsequent alteration of the bearing between the two vessels shall not make the overtaking vessel a crossing vessel within the meaning of these rules or relieve her of the duty of keeping clear of the overtaken vessel until she is finally past and clear.

Rule 13 clearly defines the overtaking situation. The overtaking vessel is burdened and required to keep out of the way, while the overtaken vessel is privileged. The signals required and the conduct of vessels during the passing depends upon the geographic characteristics of the area.

Overtaking Situation in Open Waters

In open waters, the overtaken vessel is privileged and is required to maintain course and speed. She is not required to sound any signals, unless she doubts that the burdened vessel is taking sufficient action to avoid collision, in which case she sounds the doubt or danger signal of five or more short blasts.

The overtaking vessel is burdened and is required to keep out of the way until well past and clear. As she maneuvers to keep clear of the overtaken vessel, she sounds the appropriate signals: one short blast if she turns right; two short blasts if she turns left. If she does not alter course during the passing, no signals will be sounded. Each maneuver should be accompanied by signals as long as the overtaken vessel is in sight (*see* Figure 64).

Overtaking Situation in Restricted Waters

"In a narrow channel or fairway when overtaking can take place only if the vessel to be overtaken has to take action to permit safe passing, the vessel intending to overtake shall indicate her intention by sounding" the following signals on her whistle:

—two prolonged blasts followed by one short blast to mean "I intend to overtake you on your starboard side";

—two prolonged blasts followed by two short blasts to mean "I intend to overtake you on your port side."

The vessel to be overtaken shall, if in agreement, sound the following signal on her whistle: one prolonged, one short, one prolonged, and one short, in that order (International Code group "Charlie" meaning "affirmative"). The overtaken vessel shall then take steps to permit safe passing.

If the overtaken vessel is not in agreement, she may sound instead the doubt (danger) signal of five or more short blasts. The overtaking vessel should not attempt passing until an agreement is reached, nor does agreement relieve her of her obligation to keep out of the way until well past and clear.

MEETING SITUATION

Rule 14 — Head-On Situation

(a) When two power-driven vessels are meeting on reciprocal or nearly reciprocal courses so as to involve risk of collision each shall alter her course to starboard so that each shall pass on the port side of the other.

(b) Such a situation shall be deemed to exist when a vessel sees the other ahead or nearly ahead and by night she could see the masthead lights of the other in a line or nearly in a line and/or both sidelights and by day she observes the corresponding aspect of the other vessel.

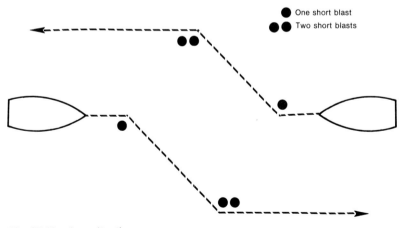

● One short blast
●● Two short blasts

Fig. 65 Head-on situation.

(c) When a vessel is in any doubt as to whether such a situation exists she shall assume that it does exist and act accordingly.

In a "head-on situation" both vessels are burdened and required to alter course to starboard in order to pass port to port. A guideline for determining if a meeting situation exists is to consider an approaching vessel "nearly ahead" if she is within one point of the bow, but if there is any doubt, assume that it is a meeting situation.

The International Rules make no mention of a starboard to starboard passage, which implies that such a passage is only proper when there is no risk of collision.

Both vessels are required to sound the appropriate maneuvering signals while they remain in sight of each other: one short blast when turning right, two short blasts when turning left, or three short blasts if backing down (although alteration of course is normally the most effective action in a meeting situation).

If vessels can pass safely port to port with no course change and without backing down, no signals are sounded.

CROSSING SITUATION

Rule 15 — Crossing Situation
When two power-driven vessels are crossing so as to involve risk of collision, the vessel which has the other on her own starboard side shall keep out of the way and shall, if the circumstances of the case admit, avoid crossing ahead of the other vessel.

A crossing situation is any situation which is neither an overtaking nor a meeting situation. In

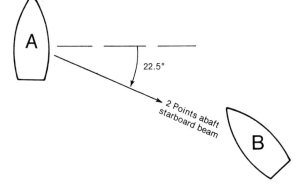

Fig. 66 Crossing or overtaking situation?

Figure 66, if vessel B is in any doubt as to whether she is overtaking or crossing, she should assume that she is overtaking and keep out of the way.

In Figure 67, if vessel B is in any doubt as to whether she is crossing or meeting, she should assume that she is meeting and alter course to starboard for a port to port passing.

In a crossing situation, the vessel which has the other on her own starboard side is burdened, and is required to sound the appropriate one, two, or three short blasts as she maneuvers to keep out of the way.

A burdened vessel taking avoiding action by turning left should not cross the projected course of the privileged vessel. If a burdened vessel can keep out of the way by slowing or stopping her engines, she sounds no signals.

The privileged vessel in a crossing situation is required to maintain course and speed. The privileged vessel can depart from the requirement to maintain course and speed under the following circumstances laid down in Rule 17:

1. The privileged vessel *may* take action to avoid collision by her maneuver alone, as soon as it becomes apparent to her that the burdened vessel is not taking appropriate action in compliance with these rules. The privileged vessel shall, if the circumstances of the case admit, not alter course to port for a vessel on her own port side.

2. When, from any cause, the privileged vessel finds herself so close that collision cannot be avoided by the action of the burdened vessel alone (i.e., she is in extremis), she *shall* take such action as will best

Fig. 67 Crossing or meeting situation?

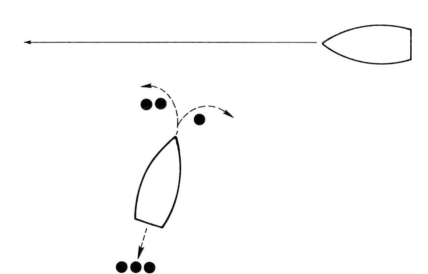

Fig. 68 Crossing situation.

aid to avoid collision. If the privileged vessel departs from the requirement to maintain course and speed, she must accompany all maneuvers, including a maneuver in extremis, with the appropriate one-, two-, or three-short-blast signals.

NARROW CHANNELS

Vessels Must Keep to the Right in a Channel (excerpt from Rule 9)

A vessel proceeding along the course of a narrow channel or fairway shall keep as near to the outer limit of the channel or fairway which lies on her starboard side as is safe and practicable.

Bend Signal (Rules 9 (f) and 34 (e))

"A vessel nearing a bend or an area of a narrow channel or fairway where other vessels may be obscured by an intervening obstruction shall navigate with particular alertness and caution and shall sound" one prolonged blast. Such signal shall be answered with a prolonged blast by any approaching vessel that may be within hearing around the bend or behind the intervening obstruction. (Note that the signal is not limited to a power-driven vessel.)

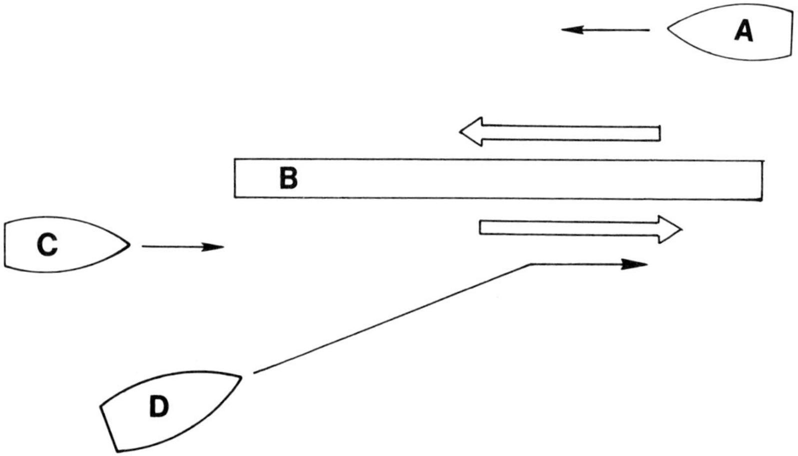

TRAFFIC SEPARATION SCHEMES (Rule 10)

(a) This rule applies to traffic separation schemes adopted by the organization [IMCO].

(b) A vessel using a traffic separation scheme shall:

(i)   proceed in the appropriate traffic lane in

Fig. 69 Traffic-separation schemes.

the general direction of traffic flow for that lane [vessel A];

(ii) so far as practicable, keep clear of a traffic separation line or separation zone [B];

(iii) normally join or leave a traffic lane at the termination of the lane [vessel C], but when joining or leaving from the side shall do so at as small an angle to the general direction of traffic flow as practicable [vessel D].

(c) A vessel shall so far as practicable avoid crossing traffic lanes, but if obliged to do so shall cross as nearly as practicable at right angles to the general direction of traffic flow.

(d) Inshore traffic zones shall not normally be used by through traffic which can safely use the appropriate traffic lane within the adjacent traffic separation scheme.

(e) A vessel, other than a crossing vessel, shall not normally enter a separation zone or cross a separation line except:

(i) in cases of emergency to avoid immediate danger;

(ii) to engage in fishing within a separation zone.

(f) A vessel navigating in areas near the terminations of traffic separation schemes shall do so with particular caution.

(g) A vessel shall so far as practicable avoid anchoring in a traffic separation scheme or in areas near its terminations.

(h) A vessel not using a traffic separation scheme shall avoid it by as wide a margin as is practicable.

(i) A vessel engaged in fishing shall not impede the passage of any vessel following a traffic lane.

(j) A vessel of less than 20 metres in length or a sailing vessel shall not impede the safe passage of a power-driven vessel following a traffic lane.

5 Law in Fog and Restricted Visibility

The International Rules that govern a vessel "navigating in or near an area of restricted visibility" are concerned with the following general types of requirements:

1. Proceeding at a "safe speed adapted to the prevailing circumstances and conditions of restricted visibility."

2. Obtaining early warning of risk of collision by maintaining a proper lookout by sight, hearing, radar, and any other available means.

3. Avoiding action when an approaching vessel is detected only on radar.

4. Avoiding action when a fog signal is heard from a vessel that has not been visually sighted.

5. Sounding the prescribed fog signals.

Rule 6 — Safe Speed

Every vessel shall at all times proceed at a safe speed so that she can take proper and effective action to avoid collision and be stopped within a distance appropriate to the prevailing circumstances and conditions.

In determining a safe speed the following factors shall be among those taken into account:

(a) By all vessels:

(i) the state of visibility;

(ii) the traffic density including concentrations of fishing vessels or any other vessels;

(iii) the manoeuvrability of the vessel with special reference to stopping distance and turning ability in the prevailing conditions;

(iv) at night the presence of background light such as from shore lights or from back scatter of her own lights;

(v) the state of wind, sea and current, and the proximity of navigational hazards;

(vi) the draught in relation to the available depth of water.

(b) Additionally, by vessels with operational radar:

(i) the characteristics, efficiency and limitations of the radar equipment;

(ii) any constraints imposed by the radar range scale in use;

(iii) the effect on radar detection of the sea state, weather and other sources of interference;

(iv) the possibility that small vessels, ice and other floating objects may not be detected by radar at an adequate range;

(v) the number, location and movement of vessels detected by radar;

(vi) the more exact assessment of the visibility that may be possible when radar is used to determine the range of vessels or other objects in the vicinity.

EARLY WARNING OF RISK OF COLLISION

Rule 5 — Lookout

Every vessel shall at all times maintain a proper lookout by sight and hearing as well as by all available means appropriate in the prevailing circumstances and conditions so as to make a full appraisal of the situation and of the risk of collision.

Rule 7 — Risk of Collision

(a) Every vessel shall use all available means appropriate to the prevailing circumstances and conditions to determine if risk of collision exists. If there is any doubt such risk shall be deemed to exist.

(b) Proper use shall be made of radar equipment if fitted and operational, including long-range scanning to obtain early warning of risk of collision and radar plotting or equivalent systematic observation of detected objects.

(c) Assumptions shall not be made on the basis of scanty information, especially scanty radar information.

(d) In determining if risk of collision exists the following considerations shall be among those taken into account:

(i) such risk shall be deemed to exist if the compass bearing of an approaching vessel does not appreciably change;

(ii) such risk may sometimes exist even when an appreciable bearing change is evident, particularly when approaching a very large vessel or a tow or when approaching a vessel at close range.

Rules 5 and 7 make two facts very obvious; radar is not a substitute for a "proper lookout by sight and hearing," nor is a quick look at the radar enough. Rule 7 requires a radar plot or "equivalent systematic observation." A radar plot includes plotting directly on the scope or on a radar deflection plotter fitted over the scope. "Systematic observation" includes the plotting teams used on most naval vessels as well as computerized collision-avoidance systems which process radar bearing and range data and display information on a cathode-ray tube.

AVOIDING RADAR CONTACTS (Rule 19(d))

(d) A vessel which detects by radar alone the presence of another vessel shall determine if a close-quarters situation is developing and/or risk of collision exists. If so, she shall take avoiding action in ample time, provided that when such action consists of an alteration of course, so far as possible the following shall be avoided:

(i) an alteration of course to port for a

vessel forward of the beam, other than for a vessel being overtaken;

(ii) an alteration of course towards a vessel abeam or abaft the beam.

The requirements of Rule 8 also apply to actions taken in fog and restricted visibility:

Rule 8 — Action to Avoid Collision

(a) Any action taken to avoid collision shall, if the circumstances of the case admit, be positive, made in ample time and with due regard to the observance of good seamanship.

(b) Any alteration of course and/or speed to avoid collision shall, if the circumstances of the case admit, be large enough to be readily apparent to another vessel observing visually or by radar; a succession of small alterations of course and/or speed should be avoided.

(c) If there is sufficient sea room, alteration of course alone may be the most effective action to avoid a close-quarters situation provided that it is made in good time, is substantial and does not result in another close-quarters situation.

(d) Action taken to avoid collision with another vessel shall be such as to result in passing at a safe distance. The effectiveness of the action shall be carefully checked until the other vessel is finally past and clear.

(e) If necessary to avoid collision or allow more time to assess the situation, a vessel shall slacken her speed or take all way off by stopping or reversing her means of propulsion.

ACTIONS WHEN A FOG SIGNAL IS HEARD (Rule 19(e))

Except where it has been determined that a risk of collision does not exist, every vessel which hears

apparently forward of her beam the fog signal of another vessel, or which cannot avoid a close-quarters situation with another vessel forward of her beam, shall reduce her speed to the minimum at which she can be kept on her course. She shall if necessary take all her way off and in any event navigate with extreme caution until danger of collision is over.

This rule requires that a vessel slow down to bare steerageway whenever a fog signal is heard apparently forward of the beam, "except where it has been determined that a risk of collision does not exist." We must assume that the rule refers to the use of radar to make the determination that risk of collision does not exist. A cautionary note is appropriate here, as the process of matching radar contacts with fog signals heard is subject to error. One reason is that sound is deceptive in fog — it is very difficult to determine the direction from which a fog signal is coming. The other factor is contained in Rule 6: "the possibility that small vessels . . . may not be detected by radar at an adequate range." Under ordinary conditions, this should not be a factor with a radar of recent design. It can, however, become an important factor when the radar is in a degraded state, or in conditions of restricted visibility caused by thunderstorms which give a radar return. The possibility exists that a maneuver to avoid a radar contact may result in a turn toward the vessel whose signal was heard.

INTERNATIONAL FOG SIGNALS

The rules contain no recommendation as to what distance should be used to determine if visibility is restricted for the purpose of sounding fog signals. Textbook-writers have long recommended the required visibility of sidelights as a guideline, which is now *three miles* for vessels of 50 meters or more in length.

All the prescribed fog signals for vessels underway are given on the whistle at intervals of not more than two minutes. The signals prescribed for a vessel at anchor or aground are given on a bell, or on a bell and gong, at intervals of not more than one minute. The optional whistle signals for a pilot vessel, a vessel at anchor and a vessel aground may be sounded as required but *in addition to* the prescribed signals. The short-prolonged-short signal may be used by a vessel at anchor to give warning of her position and of the possibility of collision to an approaching vessel.

INTERNATIONAL FOG SIGNALS*

KEY: — prolonged blast, 4-6 seconds
. short blast, about one second
S distinct stroke on bell
BELL rapid ringing of bell for 5 seconds forward
GONG rapid sounding of gong for 5 seconds aft

VESSELS UNDERWAY

CATEGORY	SIGNAL given at intervals of not more than two minutes
Power-driven vessel making way through the water	—
Power-driven vessel, underway but stopped and making no way through the water	— —
Vessel not under command Vessel restricted in her ability to maneuver	— ..

VESSELS UNDERWAY

CATEGORY	SIGNAL given at intervals of not more than two minutes
Vessel constrained by her draft Sailing vessel Vessel engaged in fishing Vessel engaged in towing or pushing	— ..
Vessel towed	— ...

VESSELS NOT UNDERWAY

CATEGORY	SIGNAL	INTERVAL
Vessel at anchor: length less than 100 meters	BELL	1 minute
length 100 meters or greater	BELL/GONG	1 minute
Any vessel at anchor may, in addition, sound	. — .	As required
Vessel aground: length less than 100 meters	SSS/BELL/SSS	1 minute
length 100 meters or greater	SSS/BELL/SSS/GONG	1 minute
Any vessel aground may, in addition, sound	APPROPRIATE WHISTLE SIGNAL**	As required

*(1) Pilot vessel may in addition sound 4 short blasts as an identity signal (sound as required).

(2) A vessel of less than 12 metres in length shall not be obliged to give the above-mentioned signals but, if she does not, shall make some other efficient sound signal at intervals of not more than 2 minutes.

**See* meanings of "F", "U", and "V" in Appendix B.

6 Special Circumstances

In International Rule 2 the expression *special circumstances* is used in two ways. Paragraph (a) recognizes that special circumstances may require precautions or actions *in addition to* the specific requirements of the other rules. (Chapter 7 deals with this subject.) Paragraph (b) of the same rule, quoted below, states that special circumstances may require a *departure* from the other rules in order to avoid "immediate danger."

> (b) In construing and complying with these rules due regard shall be had to all dangers of navigation and collision and to any special circumstances, including the limitations of the vessels involved, which may make a departure from these rules necessary to avoid immediate danger.

Special circumstances refers primarily to situations which have not been provided for in the rules. It is possible, however, to consider an example where departure from a requirement of the rules is specifically provided for in the rules themselves. The privileged vessel in a crossing situation is required by Rule 17 (a) (i) to maintain course and speed. The rule goes on to describe when a vessel *may* depart from that requirement, and then de-scribes the circumstance under which she *shall* depart from that requirement:

> (ii) The latter vessel may however take action to avoid collision by her manoeuvre alone, as soon as it becomes apparent to her that the vessel required to keep out of the way is not taking appropriate action in compliance with these rules. (Rule 17 (a) (ii))

> (b) When, from any cause, the vessel required to keep her course and speed finds herself so close that collision cannot be avoided by the action of the give-way vessel alone, she shall take such action as will best aid to avoid collision. (Rule 17 (b))

Paragraph (b) of Rule 17 is an example of where action is required in extremis. Vessels are in extremis whenever they are in such close proximity, regardless of the cause, that adherence to the ordinary rules is certain to cause a collision. The rules do not tell a vessel in extremis to back down, or to turn left or right; vessels must "take such action as will best aid to avoid collision."

When it becomes apparent that a collision will occur, vessels must be maneuvered in such a way as to minimize damage and loss of life. The primary concern in a collision is to avoid striking at such an angle that the bow of one vessel cuts into the side of the other.

As previously stated, *special circumstances* refers primarily to situations which have not been provided for in the rules. One possibility is the case where three or more vessels are approaching simultaneously. A vessel in such circumstances may find herself privileged with respect to one vessel, and burdened with respect to another. She would therefore be required to maneuver with respect to one and to maintain course and speed with respect to the other — a physical impossibility.

It may happen that two approaching vessels are both "restricted in their ability to maneuver." If the vessels are on crossing courses, and the vessel which has the other on her own starboard hand is unable to comply with the duties of a burdened vessel, the rules for two power-driven vessels crossing would not apply — their actions would be governed by Rule 2.

In "approach situations" where one or both vessels are entering or leaving a slip, maneuvering around piers, or backing, special circumstances should be deemed to exist.

Finally, there is the possibility that two vessels might agree to a departure from the rules. Although such situations are rare when subject to the International Rules, such an agreement could conceivably be reached through radio communications.

In any situation involving special circumstances, all the vessels involved must exercise extreme caution, and take whatever action is most likely to avoid collision.

7 Good Seamanship

Chapter 6 discussed special circumstances that may require a *departure* from the other International Rules. Circumstances may also require precautions *in addition to* those specified in the rules. The responsibility to take additional precautions as dictated by the special circumstances of a particular case, or by the ordinary practice of seamen, is placed on the mariner by Rule 2(a):

> Nothing in these rules shall exonerate any vessel, or the owner, master or crew thereof, from the consequences of any neglect to comply with these rules or of the neglect of any precaution which may be required by the ordinary practice of seamen, or by the special circumstances of the case.

Many of the requirements of "good seamanship" have been included in the latest revision of the rules. Note that Section I of the Steering and Sailing Rules concerns Conduct of Vessels in *Any* Condition of Visibility. Thus, the factors discussed in Chapter 5, for determining a safe speed in fog, also must be taken into consideration in determining a safe speed in clear weather. The requirements in Rule 8, actions to avoid collision, are also typical requirements of good seamanship — action taken to avoid collision should be easily understood by an observing vessel, as well as being the action which is most likely to avoid a collision.

Rules 9 and 10 advise all vessels to avoid anchoring in a narrow channel or traffic-separation scheme, or in areas near the termination of a traffic-separation scheme.

Rule 18 requires a vessel constrained by her draft to "navigate with particular caution having full regard to her special condition."

The requirements discussed in Chapter 5, concerning the maintenance of a proper lookout by sight, hearing, radar, and any other available means, are applicable in clear weather as well as in conditions of restricted visibility. Note how Rules 5 and 7 complement each other, which is as it should be, since maintaining a proper lookout is an integral part of determining if a risk of collision exists:

Rule 5 — Lookout

Every vessel shall at all times maintain a proper lookout by sight and hearing as well as by all available means appropriate in the prevailing circumstances and conditions so as to make a full appraisal of the situation and of the risk of collision.

Rule 7 — Risk of Collision

(a) Every vessel shall use all available means appropriate to the prevailing circumstances and conditions to determine if risk of collision exists. If there is any doubt such risk shall be deemed to exist.

(b) Proper use shall be made of radar equipment if fitted and operational, including long-range scanning to obtain early warning of risk of collision and radar plotting or equivalent systematic observation of detected objects.

(c) Assumptions shall not be made on the basis of scanty information, especially scanty radar information. . . .

Generally, any condition that causes a deviation from the norm may require additional precautions. Without going into specific actions that might be required, consider the following factors which may cause additional precautions to be taken:

1. Adverse weather conditions
2. Unusual conditions of loading or trim
3. Failure or degradation of any equipment important to safe navigation
4. Traffic density
5. Proximity of navigational hazards
6. Availability of external aids to navigation
7. Transport of dangerous cargo or cargo that poses a threat to the environment.

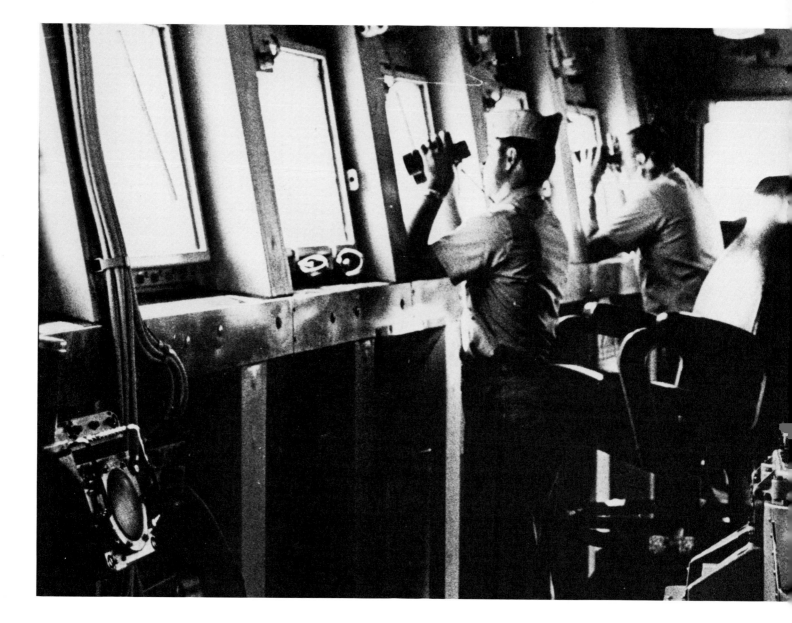

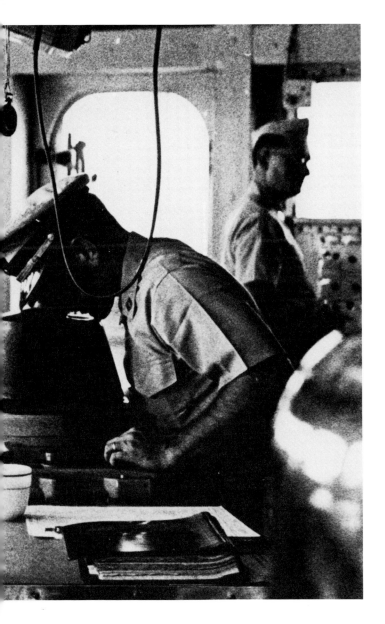

PART 3

Approach Situations
As Viewed
On Radar

Approach Situations As Viewed On Radar

Radar can be used to determine risk of collision in any condition of visibility. Holding a radar contact whose range is decreasing while the bearing remains nearly constant gives the same warning of a collision course as does a constant visual bearing. However, a series of visual bearings must always be taken when conditions permit, whether or not radar plotting is in use. A minimum amount of plotting to produce CPA range and bearing is required if a grease pencil is used directly on the radar scope.

One simple procedure is periodically to mark the position of radar contacts with a grease pencil and label with time (equal time intervals are preferred but not required). The line formed by the marks can be projected past the center of the scope as shown in Figure 70 (the direction of the line is the direction of relative motion, or DRM).

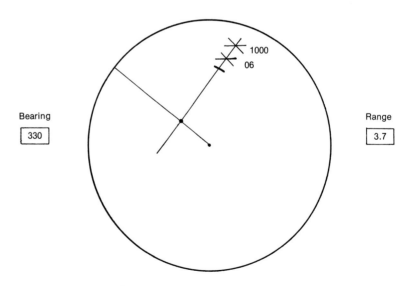

Fig. 70 Obtaining CPA bearing and range.

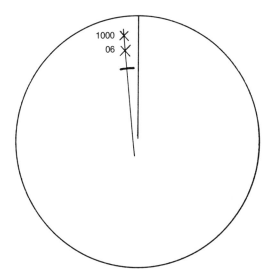

Fig. 71 Contact on a near-collision course.

CPA bearing and range can be obtained by lining up the cursor perpendicular to the contact's projected track.

In practice, radar contacts in restricted visibility are often avoided by using only the CPA information obtained from the procedures outlined above. In Figure 71, the line projected from the center of the scope represents a heading marker. A radar contact is being plotted which indicates that the vessels are on near-collision courses. With the information given, we do not readily know if the contact is headed toward us or away from us. In this example it makes little difference, as a *substantial* change of course to starboard is appropriate in either case. We must continue to watch the contact to ensure that our maneuver is having the desired effect, as illustrated in Figure 72.

In order to visualize different approach situations on radar, additional information must be considered. Take, for example, a radar contact dead ahead on a constant bearing with the range decreasing. The speed of our own vessel must be compared with the speed of relative motion (SRM) to determine if the contact is on the same course as our own vessel, on an opposite course, or dead in the water (DIW).

Consider the examples at top of following page, where our own vessel is headed north at 20 knots in each case.

In case A, the SRM is 15 knots (less than our own speed) — we are overtaking the other vessel. In case B, the SRM is 25 knots (greater than our own speed) — the vessels are meeting head and head. In

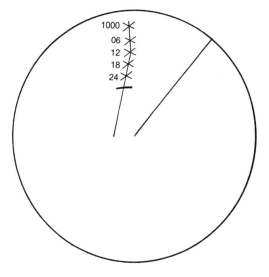

Fig. 72 Plot of contact after maneuver.

case C, the SRM is 20 knots (equal to our own speed) and the other vessel is DIW. In case D, the SRM is zero. The contact would be tracked toward the center of the scope in cases A, B, and C. If the positions are marked at equal time intervals, an estimate of the situation can be made by noting the relative closing speed.

For situations where the contact is not dead ahead, a quick glance at the radar might be deceptive. Consider a radar contact whose relative plot is crossing from right to left, as in Figure 73. At first glance it appears to be a crossing situation. However, it could also be an overtaking situation. The vectors shown illustrate two possibilities for the scope presentation (standard maneuvering board labels are employed). The vector e-m$_1$ shows a contact whose heading is only slightly left of our own, and whose speed is slightly less than our own. The vector e-m$_2$ shows a vessel crossing nearly at a right angle to our own course. The SRM is necessary to distinguish between overtaking and crossing. Notice how the SRM is relatively low in the overtaking case and increases with a greater angle between the courses.

Using the principles discussed, study the figures overleaf and determine the approach situation. In all cases, our own vessel is proceeding at a speed of 16 knots and our heading is represented by the line projected from the center of the scope. Range circles are at one-mile intervals. Use the six-minute rule to determine SRM. Solutions are shown to the right of each radar picture.

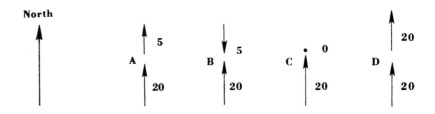

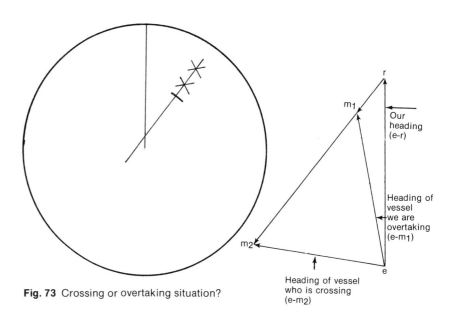

Fig. 73 Crossing or overtaking situation?

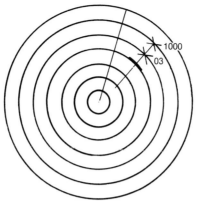

Fig. 74 Plot on radar scope.

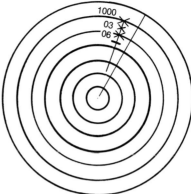

Fig. 76 Plot on radar scope.

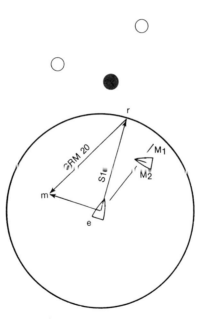

Fig. 75 Crossing situation. Aspects shown by lights above.

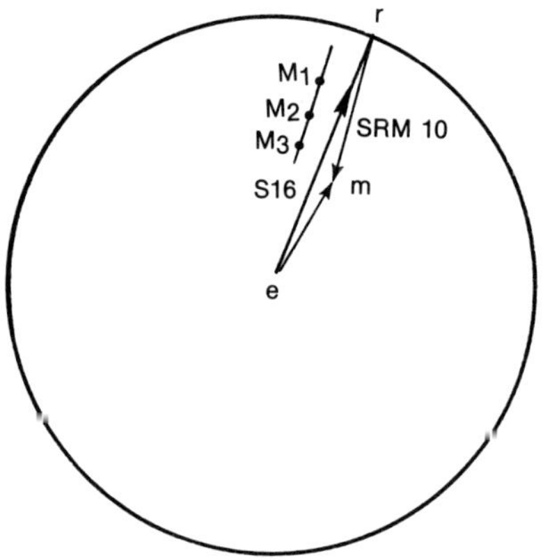

Fig. 77 Overtaking situation. Sternlight only visible.

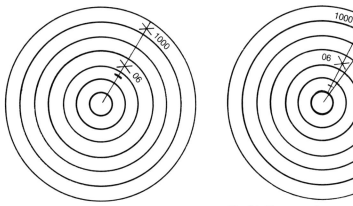

Fig. 78 Plot on radar scope.

Fig. 80 Plot on radar scope.

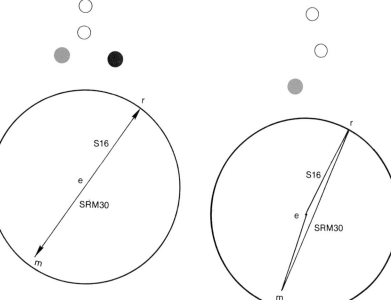

Fig. 79 Meeting situation. Aspects shown by lights above.

Fig. 81 Meeting situation. Aspects shown by lights above.

Appendixes

A Bridge-to-Bridge Radiotelephone Log Requirements*

The log of the bridge-to-bridge station required by the Vessel Bridge-to-Bridge Radiotelephone Act shall include the following entries:

(1) All radiotelephone distress and alarm signals and communications transmitted or intercepted, the text in as complete form as possible of distress messages and distress communications, and any information connected with the radio service which may appear to be of importance to maritime safety, together with the time of such observation or occurrence, the frequencies used, and the position of the ship or other mobile unit in need of assistance if this can be determined.

(2) The times when the required watch is begun, interrupted, and ended. When the required watch is interrupted for any reason, the reason for such interruption shall be stated.

(3) A daily statement concerning the operating condition of the required radiotelephone equipment, as determined either by normal communication or test communication. Where the equipment is found not to comply with the applicable provisions of this part, the log shall contain a statement as to the time the condition was discovered and the time it was brought to the master's attention.

(4) Pertinent details of all installations, service, or maintenance work performed which may affect the proper operation of the station. The entry shall be made, signed, and dated by the responsible licensed operator who supervised or performed the work, and unless such operator is employed on a full-time basis and his operator license is properly posted at a station on board the ship, such entry shall include his mail address and the class, serial number, and expiration date of his operator license.

The bridge-to-bridge log may be part of the deck log or ship station log, or the log requirements may be satisfied by automated logging.

*Title 47, Code of Federal Regulations, Section 83.368.

B Single-Letter Signals (Excerpt from H.O. 102)

May be made by any method of signaling.

A I have a diver down; keep well clear at slow speed.

*B I am taking in, or discharging, or carrying dangerous goods.

C Yes (affirmative or "The significance of the previous group should be read in the affirmative").

*D Keep clear of me; I am maneuvering with difficulty.

*E I am altering my course to starboard.

F I am disabled; communicate with me.

G I require a pilot. When made by fishing vessels operating in close proximity on the fishing grounds it means: "I am hauling nets."

*H I have a pilot on board.

*I I am altering my course to port.

J I am on fire and have dangerous cargo on board; keep well clear of me.

†K I wish to communicate with you.

L You should stop your vessel instantly.

M My vessel is stopped and making no way through the water.

*When made by sound, may only be made in compliance with the requirements of the International Regulations for Preventing Collisions at Sea.

†Has special meaning as landing signals for small boats with crews or persons in distress. (International Convention for the Safety of Life at Sea, 1960, Chapter V, Regulation 16.)

N No (negative or "The significance of the previous group should be read in the negative"). This signal may be given only visually or by sound. For voice or radio transmission the signal should be "NO."

O Man overboard.

P In harbor — All persons should report on board as the vessel is about to proceed to sea.

At sea — It may be used by fishing vessels to mean: "My nets have come fast upon an obstruction."

Q My vessel is "healthy" and I request free pratique.

*†S My engines are going astern.

*T Keep clear of me; I am engaged in pair trawling.

U You are running into danger.

V I require assistance.

W I require medical assistance

X Stop carrying out your intentions and watch for my signals.

Y I am dragging my anchor.

Z I require a tug. When made by fishing vessels operating in close proximity on the fishing grounds it means: "I am shooting nets."

C International Regulations for Preventing Collisions at Sea, 1972

PART A — GENERAL

Rule 1

Application

(a) These rules shall apply to all vessels upon the high seas and in all waters connected therewith navigable by seagoing vessels.

(b) Nothing in these rules shall interfere with the operation of special rules made by an appropriate authority for roadsteads, harbours, rivers, lakes or inland waterways connected with the high seas and navigable by seagoing vessels. Such special rules shall conform as closely as possible to these rules.

(c) Nothing in these rules shall interfere with the operation of any special rules made by the Government of any State with respect to additional station or signal lights or whistle signals for ships of war and vessels proceeding under convoy, or with respect to additional station or signal lights for fishing vessels engaged in fishing as a fleet. These additional station or signal lights or whistle signals shall, so far as possible, be such that they cannot be mistaken for any light or signal authorized elsewhere under these rules.

(d) Traffic separation schemes may be adopted by the Organization for the purpose of these rules.

(e) Whenever the Government concerned shall have determined that a vessel of special construction or purpose cannot comply fully with the provisions of any of these rules with respect to the number, position, range or arc of visibility of lights or shapes, as well as to the disposition and characteristics of sound-signalling appliances, without interfering with the special function of the vessel, such vessel shall comply with such other provisions in regard to the number, position, range or arc of visibility of lights or shapes, as well as to the disposition and characteristics of sound-signalling appliances, as her Government shall have determined to be the closest possible compliance with these rules in respect to that vessel.

Rule 2

Responsibility

(a) Nothing in these rules shall exonerate any vessel, or the owner, master or crew thereof, from the consequences of any neglect to comply with these rules or of the neglect of any precaution which may be required by the ordinary practice of seamen, or by the special circumstances of the case.

(b) In construing and complying with these rules due regard shall be had to all dangers of navigation and collision and to any special circumstances, including the limitations of the vessels involved, which may make a departure from these rules necessary to avoid immediate danger.

Rule 3

General Definitions

For the purpose of these rules, except where the context otherwise requires:

(a) The word "vessel" includes every description of water craft, including nondisplacement craft and seaplanes, used or capable of being used as a means of transportation on water.

(b) The term "power-driven vessel" means any vessel propelled by machinery.

(c) The term "sailing vessel" means any vessel under sail provided that propelling machinery, if fitted, is not being used.

(d) The term "vessel engaged in fishing" means any vessel fishing with nets, lines, trawls or other fishing apparatus which restrict manoeuvrability, but does not include a vessel fishing with trolling lines or other fishing apparatus which do not restrict manoeuvrability.

(e) The word "seaplane" includes any aircraft designed to manoeuvre on the water.

(f) The term "vessel not under command" means a vessel which through some exceptional circumstance is unable to manoeuvre as required by these rules and is therefore unable to keep out of the way of another vessel.

(g) The term "vessel restricted in her ability to manoeuvre" means a vessel which from the nature of her work is restricted in her ability to manoeuvre as required by these rules and is therefore unable to keep out of the way of another vessel.

The following vessels shall be regarded as vessels restricted in their ability to manoeuvre:

(i) a vessel engaged in laying, servicing or picking up a navigation mark, submarine cable or pipeline;

(ii) a vessel engaged in dredging, surveying or underwater operations;

(iii) a vessel engaged in replenishment or transferring persons, provisions or cargo while underway;

(iv) a vessel engaged in the launching or recovery of aircraft;

(v) a vessel engaged in minesweeping operations;

(vi) a vessel engaged in a towing operation such as severely restricts the towing vessel and her tow in their ability to deviate from their course.

(h) The term "vessel constrained by her draught" means a power-driven vessel which because of her draught in relation to the available depth of water is severely restricted in her ability to deviate from the course she is following.

(i) The word "underway" means that a vessel is not at anchor, or made fast to the shore, or aground.

(j) The words "length" and "breadth" of a vessel mean her length overall and greatest breadth.

(k) Vessels shall be deemed to be in sight of one another only when one can be observed visually from the other.

(l) The term "restricted visibility" means any condition in which visibility is restricted by fog, mist, falling snow, heavy rainstorms, sandstorms or any other similar causes.

PART B — STEERING AND SAILING RULES

SECTION I — CONDUCT OF VESSELS IN ANY CONDITION OF VISIBILITY

Rule 4

Application

Rules in this Section apply in any condition of visibility.

Rule 5

Lookout

Every vessel shall at all times maintain a proper lookout by sight and hearing as well as by all available means appropriate in the prevailing circumstances and conditions so as to make a full appraisal of the situation and of the risk of collision.

Rule 6

Safe Speed

Every vessel shall at all times proceed at a safe speed so that she can take proper and effective action to avoid collision and be stopped within a distance appropriate to the prevailing circumstances and conditions.

In determining a safe speed the following factors shall be among those taken into account:

(a) By all vessels:

(i) the state of visibility;

(ii) the traffic density including concentrations of fishing vessels or any other vessels;

(iii) the manoeuvrability of the vessel with special reference to stopping distance and turning ability in the prevailing conditions;

(iv) at night the presence of background light such as from shore lights or from back scatter of her own lights;

(v) the state of wind, sea and current, and the proximity of navigational hazards;

(vi) the draught in relation to the available depth of water.

(b) Additionally, by vessels with operational radar:

(i) the characteristics, efficiency and limitations of the radar equipment;

(ii) any constraints imposed by the radar range scale in use;

(iii) the effect on radar detection of the sea state, weather and other sources of interference;

(iv) the possibility that small vessels, ice and other floating objects may not be detected by radar at an adequate range;

(v) the number, location and movement of vessels detected by radar;

(vi) the more exact assessment of the visibility that may be possible when radar is used to determine the range of vessels or other objects in the vicinity.

Rule 7

Risk of Collision

(a) Every vessel shall use all available means appropriate to the prevailing circumstances and conditions to determine if risk of collision exists. If there is any doubt such risk shall be deemed to exist.

(b) Proper use shall be made of radar equipment if fitted and operational, including long-range scanning to obtain early warning of risk of collision and radar plotting or equivalent systematic observation of detected objects.

(c) Assumptions shall not be made on the basis of scanty information, especially scanty radar information.

(d) In determining if risk of collision exists the following considerations shall be among those taken into account:

(i) such risk shall be deemed to exist if the compass bearing of an approaching vessel does not appreciably change;

(ii) such risk may sometimes exist even when an appreciable bearing change is evident, particularly when approaching a very large vessel or a tow or when approaching a vessel at close range.

Rule 8

Action to Avoid Collision

(a) Any action taken to avoid collision shall, if the circumstances of the case admit, be positive, made in ample time and with due regard to the observance of good seamanship.

(b) Any alteration of course and/or speed to avoid collision shall, if the circumstances of the case admit, be large enough to be readily apparent to another vessel observing visually or by radar; a succession of small alterations of course and/or speed should be avoided.

(c) If there is sufficient sea room, alteration of course alone may be the most effective action to avoid a close-quarters situation provided that it is made in good time, is substantial and does not result in another close-quarters situation.

(d) Action taken to avoid collision with another vessel shall be such as to result in passing at a safe distance. The effectiveness of the action shall be carefully checked until the other vessel is finally past and clear.

(e) If necessary to avoid collision or allow more time to assess the situation, a vessel shall slacken her speed or take all way off by stopping or reversing her means of propulsion.

Rule 9

Narrow Channels

(a) A vessel proceeding along the course of a narrow channel or fairway shall keep as near to the outer limit of the channel or fairway which lies on her starboard side as is safe and practicable.

(b) A vessel of less than 20 metres in length or a sailing vessel shall not impede the passage of a vessel which can safely navigate only within a narrow channel or fairway.

(c) A vessel engaged in fishing shall not impede the passage of any other vessel navigating within a narrow channel or fairway.

(d) A vessel shall not cross a narrow channel or fairway if such crossing impedes the passage of a vessel which can safely navigate only within such channel or fairway. The latter vessel may use the sound signal prescribed in Rule 34(d) if in doubt as to the intention of the crossing vessel.

(e) (i) In a narrow channel or fairway when overtaking can take place only if the vessel to be overtaken has to take action to permit safe passing, the vessel intending to overtake shall indicate her intention by sounding the appropriate signal prescribed in Rule 34(c)(i). The vessel to be overtaken shall, if in agreement, sound the appropriate signal prescribed in Rule 34(c)(ii) and take steps to permit safe passing. If in doubt she may sound the signals prescribed in Rule 34(d).

(ii) This Rule does not relieve the overtaking vessel of her obligation under Rule 13.

(f) A vessel nearing a bend or an area of a narrow channel or fairway where other vessels may be obscured by an intervening obstruction shall navigate with particular alertness and caution and shall sound the appropriate signal prescribed in Rule 34(e).

(g) Any vessel shall, if the circumstances of the case admit, avoid anchoring in a narrow channel.

Rule 10

Traffic Separation Schemes

(a) This rule applies to traffic separation schemes adopted by the organization.

(b) A vessel using a traffic separation scheme shall:

(i) proceed in the appropriate traffic lane in the general direction of traffic flow for that lane;

(ii) so far as practicable keep clear of a traffic separation line or separation zone;

(iii) normally join or leave a traffic lane at the termination of the lane, but when joining or leaving from the side shall do so at as small an angle to the general direction of traffic flow as practicable.

(c) A vessel shall so far as practicable avoid crossing traffic lanes, but if obliged to do so shall cross as nearly as practicable at right angles to the general direction of traffic flow.

(d) Inshore traffic zones shall not normally be used by through traffic which can safely use the appropriate traffic lane within the adjacent traffic separation scheme.

(e) A vessel, other than a crossing vessel, shall not normally enter a separation zone or cross a separation line except:

(i) in cases of emergency to avoid immediate danger;

(ii) to engage in fishing within a separation zone.

(f) A vessel navigating in areas near the terminations of traffic separation schemes shall do so with particular caution.

(g) A vessel shall so far as practicable avoid anchoring in a traffic separation scheme or in areas near its terminations.

(h) A vessel not using a traffic separation scheme shall avoid it by as wide a margin as is practicable.

(i) A vessel engaged in fishing shall not impede the passage of any vessel following a traffic lane.

(j) A vessel of less than 20 metres in length or a sailing vessel shall not impede the safe passage of a power-driven vessel following a traffic lane.

SECTION II — CONDUCT OF VESSELS IN SIGHT OF ONE ANOTHER

Rule 11

Application

Rules in this section apply to vessels in sight of one another.

Rule 12

Sailing Vessels

(a) When two sailing vessels are approaching one another, so as to involve risk of collision, one of them shall keep out of the way of the other as follows:

(i) when each has the wind on a different side, the vessel which has the wind on the port side shall keep out of the way of the other;

(ii) when both have the wind on the same side, the vessel which is to windward shall keep out of the way of the vessel which is to leeward;

(iii) if a vessel with the wind on the port side sees a vessel to windward and cannot determine with certainty whether the other vessel has the wind on the port or on the starboard side, she shall keep out of the way of the other.

(b) For the purposes of this rule the windward side shall be deemed to be the side opposite to that on which the mainsail is carried or, in the case of a square-rigged vessel, the side opposite to that on which the largest fore-and-aft sail is carried.

Rule 13

Overtaking

(a) Notwithstanding anything contained in the rules of this Section any vessel overtaking any other shall keep out of the way of the vessel being overtaken.

(b) A vessel shall be deemed to be overtaking when coming up with another vessel from a direction more than 22.5 degrees abaft her beam, that is, in such a position with reference to the vessel she is overtaking, that at night she would be able to see only the sternlight of that vessel but neither of her sidelights.

(c) When a vessel is in any doubt as to whether she is overtaking another, she shall assume that this is the case and act accordingly.

(d) Any subsequent alteration of the bearing between the two vessels shall not make the overtaking vessel a crossing vessel within the meaning of these rules or relieve her of the duty of keeping clear of the overtaken vessel until she is finally past and clear.

Rule 14

Head-On Situation

(a) When two power-driven vessels are meeting on reciprocal or nearly reciprocal courses so as to involve risk of collision each shall alter her course to starboard so that each shall pass on the port side of the other.

(b) Such a situation shall be deemed to exist when a vessel sees the other ahead or nearly ahead and by night she could see the masthead lights of the other in a line or nearly in a line and/or both sidelights and by day she observes the corresponding aspect of the other vessel.

(c) When a vessel is in any doubt as to whether such a situation exists she shall assume that it does exist and act accordingly.

Rule 15

Crossing Situation

When two power-driven vessels are crossing so as to involve risk of collision, the vessel which has the other on her own starboard side shall keep out of the way and shall, if the circumstances of the case admit, avoid crossing ahead of the other vessel.

Rule 16

Action by Give-Way Vessel

Every vessel which is directed to keep out of the way of another vessel shall, so far as possible, take early and substantial action to keep well clear.

Rule 17

Action by Stand-On Vessel

(a)(i) Where one of two vessels is to keep out of the way, the other shall keep her course and speed.

(ii) The latter vessel may however take action to avoid collision by her manoeuvre alone, as soon as it becomes apparent to her that the vessel required to keep out of the way is not taking appropriate action in compliance with these rules.

(b) When, from any cause, the vessel required to keep her course and speed finds herself so close that collision cannot be avoided by the action of the give-way vessel alone, she shall take such action as will best aid to avoid collision.

(c) A power-driven vessel which takes action in a crossing situation in accordance with subparagraph (a)(ii) of this rule to avoid collision with another power-driven vessel shall, if the circumstances of the case admit, not alter course to port for a vessel on her own port side.

(d) This rule does not relieve the give-way vessel of her obligation to keep out of the way.

Rule 18

Responsibilities Between Vessels

Except where Rules 9, 10 and 13 otherwise require:

(a) A power-driven vessel underway shall keep out of the way of:

(i) a vessel not under command;

(ii) a vessel restricted in her ability to manoeuvre;

(iii) a vessel engaged in fishing;

(iv) a sailing vessel.

(b) A sailing vessel underway shall keep out of the way of:

(i) a vessel not under command;

(ii) a vessel restricted in her ability to manoeuvre;

(iii) a vessel engaged in fishing.

(c) A vessel engaged in fishing when underway shall, so far as possible, keep out of the way of:

(i) a vessel not under command;

(ii) a vessel restricted in her ability to manoeuvre.

(d)(i) Any vessel other than a vessel not under command or a vessel restricted in her ability to manoeuvre shall, if the circumstances of the case admit, avoid impeding the safe passage of a vessel constrained by her draught, exhibiting the signals in Rule 28.

(ii) A vessel constrained by her draught shall navigate with particular caution having full regard to her special condition.

(e) A seaplane on the water shall, in general, keep well clear of all vessels and avoid impeding their navigation. In circumstances, however, where risk of collision exists, she shall comply with the Rules of this Part.

SECTION III — CONDUCT OF VESSELS IN RESTRICTED VISIBILITY

Rule 19
Conduct of Vessels in Restricted Visibility

(a) This rule applies to vessels not in sight of one another when navigating in or near an area of restricted visibility.

(b) Every vessel shall proceed at a safe speed adapted to the prevailing circumstances and conditions of restricted visibility. A power-driven vessel shall have her engines ready for immediate manoeuvre.

(c) Every vessel shall have due regard to the prevailing circumstances and conditions of restricted visibility when complying with the rules of Section I of this Part.

(d) A vessel which detects by radar alone the presence of another vessel shall determine if a close-quarters situation is developing and/or risk of collision exists. If so, she shall take avoiding action in ample time, provided that when such action consists of an alteration of course, so far as possible the following shall be avoided:

(i) an alteration of course to port for a vessel forward of the beam, other than for a vessel being overtaken;

(ii) an alteration of course towards a vessel abeam or abaft the beam.

(e) Except where it has been determined that a risk of collision does not exist, every vessel which hears apparently forward of her beam the fog signal of another vessel, or which cannot avoid a close-quarters situation with another vessel forward of her beam, shall reduce her speed to the minimum at which she can be kept on her course. She shall if necessary take all her way off and in any event navigate with extreme caution until danger of collision is over.

PART C — LIGHTS AND SHAPES

Rule 20
Application

(a) Rules in this part shall be complied with in all weathers.

(b) The rules concerning lights shall be complied with from sunset to sunrise, and during such times no other lights shall be exhibited, except such lights as cannot be mistaken for the lights specified in these rules or do not impair their visibility or distinctive character, or interfere with the keeping of a proper lookout.

(c) The lights prescribed by these rules shall, if carried, also be exhibited from sunrise to sunset in restricted visibility and may be exhibited in all other circumstances when it is deemed necessary.

(d) The rules concerning shapes shall be complied with by day.

(e) The lights and shapes specified in these rules shall comply with the provisions of Annex I to these regulations.

Rule 21

Definitions

(a) "Masthead light" means a white light placed over the fore and aft centreline of the vessel showing an unbroken light over an arc of the horizon of 225 degrees and so fixed as to show the light from right ahead to 22.5 degrees abaft the beam on either side of the vessel.

(b) "Sidelights" means a green light on the starboard side and a red light on the port side each showing an unbroken light over an arc of the horizon of 112.5 degrees and so fixed as to show the light from right ahead to 22.5 degrees abaft the beam on its respective side. In a vessel of less than 20 metres in length the sidelights may be combined in one lantern carried on the fore and aft centreline of the vessel.

(c) "Sternlight" means a white light placed as nearly as practicable at the stern showing an unbroken light over an arc of the horizon of 135 degrees and so fixed as to show the light 67.5 degrees from right aft on each side of the vessel.

(d) "Towing light" means a yellow light having the same characteristics as the "sternlight" defined in paragraph (c) of this rule.

(e) "All round light" means a light showing an unbroken light over an arc of the horizon of 360 degrees.

(f) "Flashing light" means a light flashing at regular intervals at a frequency of 120 flashes or more per minute.

Rule 22

Visibility of Lights

The lights prescribed in these rules shall have an intensity as specified in Section 8 of Annex I to these regulations so as to be visible at the following minimum ranges:

(a) In vessels of 50 metres or more in length:
—a masthead light, 6 miles;
—a sidelight, 3 miles;
—a sternlight, 3 miles;
—a towing light, 3 miles;
—a white, red, green or yellow all-round light, 3 miles.

(b) In vessels of 12 metres or more in length but less than 50 metres in length:
—a masthead light, 5 miles; except that where the length of the vessel is less than 20 metres, 3 miles;
—a sidelight, 2 miles;
—a sternlight, 2 miles;
—a towing light, 2 miles;
—a white, red, green or yellow all-round light, 2 miles.

(c) In vessels of less than 12 metres in length:
—a masthead light, 2 miles;
—a sidelight, 1 mile;
—a sternlight, 2 miles;
—a towing light, 2 miles;
—a white, red, green or yellow all-round light, 2 miles.

Rule 23

Power-Driven Vessels Underway

(a) A power-driven vessel underway shall exhibit:

(i) a masthead light forward;

(ii) a second masthead light abaft of and higher than the forward one; except that a vessel of less than 50 metres in length shall not be obliged to exhibit such light but may do so;

(iii) sidelights;

(iv) a sternlight.

(b) An air-cushion vessel when operating in the non-displacement mode shall, in addition to the lights prescribed in paragraph (a) of this rule, exhibit an all-round flashing yellow light.

(c) A power-driven vessel of less than 7 metres in length and whose maximum speed does not exceed 7 knots may, in lieu of the lights prescribed in paragraph (a) of this rule, exhibit an all-round white light. Such vessel shall, if practicable, also exhibit sidelights.

Rule 24

Towing and Pushing

(a) A power-driven vessel when towing shall exhibit:

(i) instead of the light prescribed in Rule 23(a)(i), two masthead lights forward in a vertical line. When the length of the tow, measuring from the stern of the towing vessel to the after end of the tow exceeds 200 metres, three such lights in a vertical line;

(ii) sidelights;

(iii) a sternlight;

(iv) a towing light in a vertical line above the sternlight;

(v) when the length of the tow exceeds 200 metres, a diamond shape where it can best be seen.

(b) When a pushing vessel and a vessel being pushed ahead are rigidly connected in a composite unit they shall be regarded as a power-driven vessel and exhibit the lights prescribed in Rule 23.

(c) A power-driven vessel when pushing ahead or towing alongside, except in the case of a composite unit, shall exhibit:

(i) instead of the light prescribed in Rule 23(a)(i), two masthead lights forward in a vertical line;

(ii) sidelights;

(iii) a sternlight.

(d) A power-driven vessel to which paragraphs (a) and (c) of this rule apply shall also comply with Rule 23(a)(ii).

(e) A vessel or object being towed shall exhibit:

(i) sidelights;

(ii) a sternlight;

(iii) when the length of the tow exceeds 200 metres, a diamond shape where it can best be seen.

(f) Provided that any number of vessels being towed alongside or pushed in a group shall be lighted as one vessel,

(i) a vessel being pushed ahead, not being part of a composite unit, shall exhibit at the forward end, sidelights;

(ii) a vessel being towed alongside shall exhibit a sternlight and at the forward end, sidelights.

(g) Where from any sufficient cause it is impracticable for a vessel or object being towed to exhibit the lights prescribed in paragraph (e) of this rule, all possible measures shall be taken to light the vessel or object towed or at least to indicate the presence of the unlighted vessel or object.

Rule 25

Sailing Vessels Underway and Vessels Under Oars

(a) A sailing vessel underway shall exhibit:
(i) sidelights;
(ii) a sternlight.

(b) In a sailing vessel of less than 12 metres in length the lights prescribed in paragraph (a) of this rule may be combined in one lantern carried at or near the top of the mast where it can best be seen.

(c) A sailing vessel underway may, in addition to the lights prescribed in paragraph (a) of this rule, exhibit at or near the top of the mast, where they can best be seen, two all-round lights in a vertical line, the upper being red and the lower green, but these lights shall not be exhibited in conjunction with the combined lantern permitted by paragraph (b) of this rule.

(d)(i) A sailing vessel of less than 7 metres in length shall, if practicable, exhibit the lights prescribed in paragraph (a) or (b) of this rule, but if she does not, she shall have ready at hand an electric torch or lighted lantern showing a white light which shall be exhibited in sufficient time to prevent collision.

(ii) A vessel under oars may exhibit the lights prescribed in this rule for sailing vessels, but if she does not, she shall have ready at hand an electric torch or lighted lantern showing a white light which shall be exhibited in sufficient time to prevent collision.

(e) A vessel proceeding under sail when also being propelled by machinery shall exhibit forward where it can best be seen a conical shape, apex downwards.

Rule 26

Fishing Vessels

(a) A vessel engaged in fishing, whether underway or at anchor, shall exhibit only the lights and shapes prescribed in this rule.

(b) A vessel when engaged in trawling, by which is meant the dragging through the water of a dredge net or other apparatus used as a fishing appliance, shall exhibit:

(i) two all-round lights in a vertical line, the upper being green and the lower white, or a shape consisting of two cones with their apexes together in a vertical line one above the other; a vessel of less than 20 metres in length may instead of this shape exhibit a basket;

(ii) a masthead light abaft of and higher than the all-round green light; a vessel of less than 50 metres in length shall not be obliged to exhibit such a light but may do so;

(iii) when making way through the water, in addition to the lights prescribed in this paragraph, sidelights and a sternlight.

(c) A vessel engaged in fishing, other than trawling, shall exhibit:

(i) two all-round lights in a vertical line, the upper being red and the lower white, or a shape consisting of two cones with apexes together in a vertical line one above the other; a vessel of less than 20 metres in length may instead of this shape exhibit a basket;

(ii) when there is outlying gear extending more than 150 metres horizontally from the vessel, an all-round white light or a cone apex upwards in the direction of the gear;

(iii) when making way through the water, in addition to the lights prescribed in this paragraph, sidelights and a sternlight.

(d) A vessel engaged in fishing in close proximity to other vessels engaged in fishing may exhibit the additional signals described in Annex II to these regulations.

(e) A vessel when not engaged in fishing shall not exhibit the lights or shapes prescribed in this rule, but only those prescribed for a vessel of her length.

Rule 27

Vessels Not Under Command or
Restricted in their Ability to Manoeuvre

(a) A vessel not under command shall exhibit:

(i) two all-round red lights in a vertical line where they can best be seen;

(ii) two balls or similar shapes in a vertical line where they can best be seen;

(iii) when making way through the water, in addition to the lights prescribed in this paragraph, sidelights and a sternlight.

(b) A vessel restricted in her ability to manoeuvre, except a vessel engaged in minesweeping operations, shall exhibit:

(i) three all-round lights in a vertical line where they can best be seen. The highest and lowest of these lights shall be red and the middle light shall be white;

(ii) three shapes in a vertical line where they can best be seen. The highest and lowest of these shapes shall be balls and the middle one a diamond;

(iii) when making way through the water,

masthead lights, sidelights and a sternlight, in addition to the lights prescribed in subparagraph (i);

(iv) when at anchor, in addition to the lights or shapes prescribed in subparagraphs (i) and (ii), the light, lights or shape prescribed in Rule 30.

(c) A vessel engaged in a towing operation such as renders her unable to deviate from her course shall, in addition to the lights or shapes prescribed in subparagraphs (b)(i) and (ii) of this rule, exhibit the lights or shape prescribed in Rule 24(a).

(d) A vessel engaged in dredging or underwater operations, when restricted in her ability to manoeuvre, shall exhibit the lights and shapes prescribed in paragraph (b) of this rule and shall in addition, when an obstruction exists, exhibit:

(i) two all-round red lights or two balls in a vertical line to indicate the side on which the obstruction exists;

(ii) two all-round green lights or two diamonds in a vertical line to indicate the side on which another vessel may pass;

(iii) when making way through the water, in addition to the lights prescribed in this paragraph, masthead lights, sidelights and a sternlight;

(iv) a vessel to which this paragraph applies when at anchor shall exhibit the lights or shapes prescribed in subparagraphs (i) and (ii) instead of the lights or shape prescribed in Rule 30.

(e) Whenever the size of a vessel engaged in diving operations makes it impracticable to exhibit the shapes prescribed in paragraph (d) of this rule, a rigid replica of the International Code flag "A" not less than 1 metre in height shall be exhibited. Measures shall be taken to ensure all-round visibility.

(f) A vessel engaged in minesweeping operations shall, in addition to the lights prescribed for a power-driven vessel in Rule 23, exhibit three all-round green lights or three balls. One of these lights or shapes shall be exhibited at or near the foremast head and one at each end of the fore yard. These lights or shapes indicate that it is dangerous for another vessel to approach closer than 1,000 metres astern or 500 metres on either side of the minesweeper.

(g) Vessels of less than 7 metres in length shall not be required to exhibit the lights prescribed in this rule.

(h) The signals prescribed in this rule are not signals of vessels in distress and requiring assistance. Such signals are contained in Annex IV to these regulations.

Rule 28

Vessels Constrained by their Draught

A vessel constrained by her draught may, in addition to the lights prescribed for power-driven vessels in Rule 23, exhibit where they can best be seen three all-round red lights in a vertical line, or a cylinder.

Rule 29

Pilot Vessels

(a) A vessel engaged on pilotage duty shall exhibit:

(i) at or near the masthead, two all-round lights in a vertical line, the upper being white and the lower red;

(ii) when underway, in addition, sidelights and a sternlight;

(iii) when at anchor, in addition to the lights prescribed in subparagraph (i), the anchor light, lights or shape.

(b) A pilot vessel when not engaged on pilotage duty shall exhibit the lights or shapes prescribed for a similar vessel of her length.

Rule 30

Anchored Vessels and Vessels Aground

(a) A vessel at anchor shall exhibit where it can best be seen:

(i) in the fore part, an all-round white light or one ball;

(ii) at or near the stern and at a lower level than the light prescribed in subparagraph (i), an all-round white light.

(b) A vessel of less than 50 metres in length may exhibit an all-round white light where it can best be seen instead of the lights prescribed in paragraph (a) of this rule.

(c) A vessel at anchor may, and a vessel of 100 metres and more in length shall, also use the available working or equivalent lights to illuminate her decks.

(d) A vessel aground shall exhibit the lights prescribed in paragraph (a) or (b) of this rule and in addition, where they can best be seen:

(i) two all-round red lights in a vertical line;

(ii) three balls in a vertical line.

(e) A vessel of less than 7 metres in length, when at anchor or aground, not in or near a narrow channel, fairway or anchorage, or where other vessels normally navigate, shall not be required to exhibit the lights or shapes prescribed in paragraphs (a), (b) or (d) of this rule.

Rule 31

Seaplanes

Where it is impracticable for a seaplane to exhibit lights and shapes of the characteristics or in the positions prescribed in the rules of this part she shall exhibit lights and shapes as closely similar in characteristics and position as is possible.

PART D — SOUND AND LIGHT SIGNALS

Rule 32

Definitions

(a) The word "whistle" means any sound signalling appliance capable of producing the prescribed blasts and which complies with the specifications in Annex III to these regulations.

(b) The term "short blast" means a blast of about one second's duration.

(c) The term "prolonged blast" means a blast of from four to six seconds' duration.

Rule 33

Equipment for Sound Signals

(a) A vessel of 12 metres or more in length shall be provided with a whistle and a bell and a vessel of 100 metres or more in length shall, in addition, be provided with a gong, the tone and sound of which cannot be confused with that of the bell. The whistle, bell and gong shall comply with the specifications in Annex III to these regulations. The bell or gong or both may be replaced by other equipment having the same respective sound characteris-

tics, provided that manual sounding of the required signals shall always be possible.

(b) A vessel of less than 12 metres in length shall not be obliged to carry the sound signalling appliances prescribed in paragraph (a) of this rule but if she does not, she shall be provided with some other means of making an efficient sound signal.

Rule 34

Manoeuvring and Warning Signals

(a) When vessels are in sight of one another, a power-driven vessel underway, when manoeuvring as authorized or required by these rules, shall indicate that manoeuvre by the following signals on her whistle:

—one short blast to mean "I am altering my course to starboard";

—two short blasts to mean "I am altering my course to port";

three short blasts to mean "I am operating astern propulsion".

(b) Any vessel may supplement the whistle signals prescribed in paragraph (a) of this rule by light signals, repeated as appropriate, whilst the manoeuvre is being carried out.

(i) these light signals shall have the following significance:

—one flash to mean "I am altering my course to starboard";

—two flashes to mean "I am altering my course to port";

—three flashes to mean "I am operating astern propulsion";

(ii) the duration of each flash shall be about one second, the interval between flashes shall be about one second, and the interval between successive signals shall be not less than ten seconds;

    (iii) the light used for this signal shall, if fitted, be an all-round white light, visible at a minimum range of 5 miles, and shall comply with the provisions of Annex I.

(c) When in sight of one another in a narrow channel or fairway:

    (i) a vessel intending to overtake another shall in compliance with Rule 9(e)(i) indicate her intention by the following signals on her whistle:

—two prolonged blasts followed by one short blast to mean "I intend to overtake you on your starboard side";

—two prolonged blasts followed by two short blasts to mean "I intend to overtake you on your port side."

    (ii) the vessel about to be overtaken when acting in accordance with Rule 9(e)(i) shall indicate her agreement by the following signal on her whistle:

—one prolonged, one short, one prolonged and one short blast, in that order.

(d) When vessels in sight of one another are approaching each other and from any cause either vessel fails to understand the intentions or actions of the other, or is in doubt whether sufficient action is being taken by the other to avoid collision, the vessel in doubt shall immediatley indicate such doubt by giving at least five short and rapid blasts on the whistle. Such signal may be supplemented by a light signal of at least five short and rapid flashes.

(e) A vessel nearing a bend or an area of a channel or fairway where other vessels may be obscured by an intervening obstruction shall sound one prolonged blast. Such signal shall be answered with a prolonged blast by any approaching vessel that may be within hearing around the bend or behind the intervening obstruction.

(f) If whistles are fitted on a vessel at a distance apart of more than 100 metres, one whistle only shall be used for giving manoeuvring and warning signals.

Rule 35
Sound Signals in Restricted Visibility

In or near an area of restricted visibility, whether by day or night, the signals prescribed in this rule shall be used as follows:

(a) A power-driven vessel making way through the water shall sound at intervals of not more than 2 minutes one prolonged blast.

(b) A power-driven vessel underway but stopped and making no way through the water shall sound at intervals of not more than 2 minutes two prolonged blasts in succession with an interval of about 2 seconds between them.

(c) A vessel not under command, a vessel restricted in her ability to manoeuvre, a vessel constrained by her draught, a sailing vessel, a vessel engaged in fishing and a vessel engaged in towing or pushing another vessel shall, instead of the signals prescribed in paragraphs (a) (b) of this rule, sound at intervals of not more than 2 minutes three blasts in succession, namely one prolonged followed by two short blasts.

(d) A vessel towed or if more than one vessel is towed the last vessel of the tow, if manned, shall at intervals of not more than 2 minutes sound four blasts in succession, namely one prolonged followed by three short blasts. When practicable, this signal shall be made immediately after the signal made by the towing vessel.

(e) When a pushing vessel and a vessel being pushed ahead are rigidly connected in a composite unit they shall be regarded as a power-driven vessel and shall give the signals prescribed in paragraphs (a) or (b) of this rule.

(f) A vessel at anchor shall at intervals of not more than one minute ring the bell rapidly for about 5 seconds. In a vessel of 100 metres or more in length the bell shall be sounded in the forepart of the vessel and immediately after the ringing of the bell the gong shall be sounded rapidly for about 5 seconds in the after part of the vessel. A vessel at anchor may in addition sound three blasts in succession, namely one short, one prolonged and one short blast, to give warning of her position and of the possibility of collision to an approaching vessel.

(g) A vessel aground shall give the bell signal and if required the gong signal prescribed in paragraph (f) of this rule and shall, in addition, give three separate and distinct strokes on the bell immediately before and after the rapid ringing of the bell. A vessel aground may in addition sound an appropriate whistle signal.

(h) A vessel of less than 12 metres in length shall not be obliged to give the above-mentioned signals but, if she does not, shall make some other efficient sound signal at intervals of not more than 2 minutes.

(i) A pilot vessel when engaged on pilotage duty may in addition to the signals prescribed in paragraphs (a), (b) or (f) of this rule sound an identity signal consisting of four short blasts.

Rule 36
Signals to Attract Attention

If necessary to attract the attention of another vessel, any vessel may make light or sound signals that cannot be mistaken for any signal authorized elsewhere in these rules, or may direct the beam of her searchlight in the direction of the danger, in such a way as not to embarrass any vessel.

Rule 37
Distress Signals

When a vessel is in distress and requires assistance she shall use or exhibit the signals prescribed in Annex IV to these regulations.

PART E — EXEMPTIONS

Rule 38
Exemptions

Any vessel (or class of vessels) provided that she complies with the requirements of the International Regulations for Preventing Collisions at Sea, 1960, the keel of which is laid or which is at a corresponding stage of construction before the entry into force of these regulations may be exempted from compliance therewith as follows:

(a) The installation of lights with ranges prescribed in Rule 22, until four years after the date of entry into force of these regulations.

(b) The installation of lights with colour specifications as prescribed in Section 7 of Annex I to these regulations, until four years after the date of entry into force of these regulations.

(c) The repositioning of lights as a result of conversion from Imperial to metric units and rounding off measurement figures, permanent exemption.

(d)(i) The repositioning of masthead lights on vessels of less than 150 metres in length, resulting from the prescriptions of Section 3(a) of Annex I, permanent exemption.

(ii) The repositioning of masthead lights on vessels of 150 metres or more in length, resulting from the prescriptions of Section 3(a) of Annex I to these regulations, until 9 years after the date of entry into force of these regulations.

(e) The repositioning of masthead lights resulting from the prescriptions of Section 2(b) of Annex I, until 9 years after the date of entry into force of these regulations.

(f) The repositioning of sidelights resulting from the prescriptions of Sections 2(g) and 3(b) of Annex I, until 9 years after the date of entry into force of these regulations.

(g) The requirements for sound signal appliances prescribed in Annex III, until 9 years after the date of entry into force of these regulations.

ANNEX I

POSITIONING AND TECHNICAL DETAILS OF LIGHTS AND SHAPES

1. *Definition*

The term "height above the hull" means height above the uppermost continuous deck.

2. *Vertical Positioning and Spacing of Lights*

(a) On a power-driven vessel of 20 metres or more in length the masthead lights shall be placed as follows:

(i) the forward masthead light, or if only one masthead light is carried, then that light, at a height above the hull of not less than 6 metres, and, if the breadth of the vessel exceeds 6 metres, then at a height above the hull not less than such breadth, so however that the light need not be placed at a greater height above the hull than 12 metres;

(ii) when two masthead lights are carried the after one shall be at least 4.5 metres vertically higher than the forward one.

(b) The vertical separation of masthead lights of power-driven vessels shall be such that in all normal conditions of trim the after light will be seen over and separate from the forward light at a distance of 1000 metres from the stem when viewed from sea level.

(c) The masthead light of a power-driven vessel of 12 metres but less than 20 metres in length shall be placed at a height above the gunwale of not less than 2.5 metres.

(d) A power-driven vessel of less than 12 metres in length may carry the uppermost light at a height of less than 2.5 metres above the gunwale. When however a masthead light is carried in addition to sidelights and a sternlight, then such masthead light shall be carried at least 1 metre higher than the sidelights.

(e) One of the two or three masthead lights prescribed for a power-driven vessel when engaged in towing or pushing another vessel shall be placed in the same position as the forward masthead light of a power-driven vessel.

(f) In all circumstances the masthead light or lights shall be so placed as to be above and clear of all other lights and obstructions.

(g) The sidelights of a power-driven vessel shall be placed at a height above the hull not greater than three quarters of that of the forward masthead light. They shall not be so low as to be interfered with by deck lights.

(h) The sidelights, if in a combined lantern and carried on a power-driven vessel of less than 20 metres in length, shall be placed not less than 1 metre below the masthead light.

(i) When the rules prescribe two or three lights to be carried in a vertical line, they shall be spaced as follows:

(i) on a vessel of 20 metres in length or more such lights shall be spaced not less than 2 metres apart, and the lowest of these lights shall, except where a towing light is required, not be less than 4 metres above the hull;

(ii) on a vessel of less than 20 metres in length such lights shall be spaced not less than 1 metre apart and the lowest of these lights shall, except where a towing light is required, not be less than 2 metres above the gunwale;

(iii) when three lights are carried they shall be equally spaced.

(j) The lower of the two all-round lights prescribed for a fishing vessel when engaged in fishing shall be at a height above the sidelights not less

than twice the distance between the two vertical lights.

(k) The forward anchor light, when two are carried, shall not be less than 4.5 metres above the after one. On a vessel of 50 metres or more in length this forward anchor light shall not be less than 6 metres above the hull.

3. *Horizontal Positioning and Spacing of Lights*

(a) When two masthead lights are prescribed for a power-driven vessel, the horizontal distance between them shall not be less than one half of the length of the vessel but need not be more than 100 metres. The forward light shall be placed not more than one quarter of the length of the vessel from the stem.

(b) On a vessel of 20 metres or more in length the sidelights shall not be placed in front of the forward masthead lights. They shall be placed at or near the side of the vessel.

4. *Details of Location of Direction-Indicating Lights for Fishing Vessels, Dredgers and Vessels Engaged in Underwater Operations*

(a) The light indicating the direction of the outlying gear from a vessel engaged in fishing as prescribed in Rule 26(c)(ii) shall be placed at a horizontal distance of not less than 2 metres and not more than 6 metres away from the two all-round red and white lights. This light shall be placed not higher than the all-round white light prescribed in Rule 26(c)(i) and not lower than the sidelights.

(b) The lights and shapes on a vessel engaged in dredging or underwater operations to indicate the obstructed side and/or the side on which it is safe to pass, as prescribed in Rule 27(d)(i) and (ii), shall be placed at the maximum practical horizontal distance, but in no case less than 2 metres, from the lights or shapes prescribed in Rule 27(b)(i) and (ii). In no case shall the upper of these lights or shapes be at a greater height than the lower of the three lights or shapes prescribed in Rule 27(b)(i) and (ii).

5. Screens for Sidelights

The sidelights shall be fitted with inboard screens painted matt black, and meeting the requirements of Section 9 of this Annex. With a combined lantern, using a single vertical filament and a very narrow division between the green and red sections, external screens need not be fitted.

6. Shapes

(a) Shapes shall be black and of the following sizes:

    (i) a ball shall have a diameter of not less than 0.6 metre;

    (ii) a cone shall have a base diameter of not less than 0.6 metre and a height equal to its diameter;

    (iii) a cylinder shall have a diameter of at least 0.6 metre and a height of twice its diameter;

    (iv) a diamond shape shall consist of two cones as defined in (ii) above having a common base.

(b) The vertical distance between shapes shall be at least 1.5 metre.

(c) In a vessel of less than 20 metres in length shapes of lesser dimensions but commensurate with the size of the vessel may be used and the distance apart may be correspondingly reduced.

7. Colour Specification of Lights

The chromaticity of all navigation lights shall conform to the following standards, which lie within the boundaries of the area of the diagram specified for each colour by the International Commisson on Illumination (CIE).

The boundaries of the area for each colour are given by indicating the corner co-ordinates, which are as follows:

(i) *White:*

x	0.525	0.525	0.452	0.310	0.310	0.443
y	0.382	0.440	0.440	0.348	0.283	0.382

(ii) *Green:*

x	0.028	0.009	0.300	0.203
y	0.385	0.723	0.511	0.356

(iii) *Red:*

x	0.680	0.660	0.735	0.721
y	0.320	0.320	0.265	0.259

(iv) *Yellow:*

x	0.612	0.618	0.575	0.575
y	0.382	0.382	0.425	0.406

8. Intensity of Lights

(a) The minimum luminous intensity of lights shall be calculated by using the formula:

$$I = 3.43 \times 10^6 \times T \times D^2 \times K^{-D}$$

where I is luminous intensity in candelas under service conditions,

    T is threshold factor 2×10^{-7} lux,

    D is range of visibility (luminous range) of the light in nautical miles,

    K is atmospheric transmissivity. For prescribed lights the value of K shall be 0.8, corresponding to a meteorological visibility of approximately 13 nautical miles.

(b) A selection of figures derived from the formula is given in the following table:

Range of visibility (luminous range) of light in nautical miles D	Luminous intensity of light in candelas for K = 0.8 I
1	0.9
2	4.3
3	12.0
4	27.0
5	52.0
6	94.0

Note: The maximum luminous intensity of navigation lights should be limited to avoid undue glare.

9. *Horizontal Sectors*

(a)(i) In the forward direction, sidelights as fitted on the vessel must show the minimum required intensities. The intensities must decrease to reach practical cut-off between 1 degree and 3 degrees outside the prescribed sectors.

(ii) For sternlights and masthead lights and at 22.5 degrees abaft the beam for sidelights, the minimum required intensities shall be maintained over the arc of the horizon up to 5 degrees within the limits of the sectors prescribed in Rule 21. From 5 degrees within the prescribed sectors the intensity may decrease by 50 percent up to the prescribed limits; it shall decrease steadily to reach practical cut-off at not more than 5 degrees outside the prescribed limits.

(b) All-round lights shall be so located as not to be obscured by masts, topmasts or structures within angular sectors of more than 6 degrees, except anchor lights, which need not be placed at an impracticable height above the hull.

10. *Vertical Sectors*

(a) The vertical sectors of electric lights, with the exception of lights on sailing vessels shall ensure that:

(i) at least the required minimum intensity is maintained at all angles from 5 degrees above to 5 degrees below the horizontal;

(ii) at least 60 percent of the required minimum intensity is maintained from 7.5 degrees above to 7.5 degrees below the horizontal.

(b) In the case of sailing vessels the vertical sectors of electric lights shall ensure that:

(i) at least the required minimum intensity is maintained at all angles from 5 degrees above to 5 degrees below the horizontal;

(ii) at least 50 percent of the required minimum intensity is maintained from 25 degrees above to 25 degrees below the horizontal.

(c) In the case of lights other than electric these specifications shall be met as closely as possible.

11. *Intensity of Non-Electric Lights*

Nonelectric lights shall so far as practicable comply with the minimum intensities, as specified in the Table given in Section 8 of this Annex.

12. *Manoeuvring Light*

Notwithstanding the provisions of paragraph

2(f) of this Annex the manoeuvring light described in Rule 34(b) shall be placed in the same fore and aft vertical plane as the masthead light or lights and, where practicable, at a minimum height of 2 metres vertically above the forward masthead light, provided that it shall be carried not less than 2 metres vertically above or below the after masthead light. On a vessel where only one masthead light is carried the manoeuvring light, if fitted, shall be carried where it can best be seen, not less than 2 metres vertically apart from the masthead light.

13. *Approval*

The construction of lanterns and shapes and the installation of lanterns on board the vessel shall be to the satisfaction of the appropriate authority of the State where the vessel is registered.

ANNEX II

ADDITIONAL SIGNALS FOR FISHING VESSELS FISHING IN CLOSE PROXIMITY

1. *General*

The lights mentioned herein shall, if exhibited in pursuance of Rule 26(d), be placed where they can best be seen. They shall be at least 0.9 metre apart but at a lower level than lights prescribed in Rule 26(b)(i) and (c)(i). The lights shall be visible all round the horizon at a distance of at least 1 mile but at a lesser distance than the lights prescribed by these rules for fishing vessels.

2. *Signals for Trawlers*

(a) Vessels when engaged in trawling, whether using demersal or pelagic gear, may exhibit:
(i) when shooting their nets: two white lights in a vertical line;
(ii) when hauling their nets: one white light over one red light in a vertical line;
(iii) when the net has come fast upon an obstruction: two red lights in a vertical line.
(b) Each vessel engaged in pair trawling may exhibit:
(i) by night, a searchlight directed forward and in the direction of the other vessel of the pair;
(ii) when shooting or hauling their nets or when their nets have come fast upon an obstruction, the lights prescribed in 2(a) above.

3. *Signals for Purse Seiners*

Vessels engaged in fishing with purse seine gear may exhibit two yellow lights in a vertical line. These lights shall flash alternately every second and with equal light and occultation duration. These lights may be exhibited only when the vessel is hampered by its fishing gear.

ANNEX III

TECHNICAL DETAILS OF SOUND SIGNAL APPLIANCES

1. *Whistles*

(a) *Frequencies and range of audibility*. The

fundamental frequency of the signal shall lie within the range 70-700 Hz.

The range of audibility of the signal from a whistle shall be determined by those frequencies, which may include the fundamental and/or one or more higher frequencies, which lie within the range 180-700 Hz (±1 percent) and which provide the sound pressure levels specified in paragraph 1(c) below.

(b) *Limits of fundamental frequencies.* To ensure a wide variety of whistle characteristics, the fundamental frequency of a whistle shall be between the following limits:

    (i) 70-200 Hz, for a vessel 200 metres or more in length;

    (ii) 130-350 Hz, for a vessel 75 metres but less than 200 metres in length;

    (iii) 250-700 Hz, for a vessel less than 75 metres in length.

(c) *Sound signal intensity and range of audibility.* A whistle fitted in a vessel shall provide, in the direction of maximum intensity of the whistle and at a distance of 1 metre from it, a sound pressure level in at least one 1/3-octave band within the range of frequencies 180-700 Hz (±1 percent) of not less than the appropriate figure given in the table below.

Length of vessel in metres	1/3d-octave band level at 1 metre in dB referred to 2×10^{-5} N/m²	Audibility range in nautical miles
200 or more	143	2
75 but less than 200....	138	1.5
20 but less than 75.....	130	1
Less than 20	120	0.5

The range of audibility in the table above is for information and is approximately the range at which a whistle may be heard on its forward axis with 90 percent probability in conditions of still air on board a vessel having average background noise level at the listening posts (taken to be 68dB in the octave band centred on 250 Hz and 63 dB in the octave band centred on 500 Hz).

In practice the range at which a whistle may be heard is extremely variable and depends critically on weather conditions; the values given can be regarded as typical but under conditions of strong wind or high ambient noise level at the listening post the range may be much reduced.

(d) *Directional properties.* The sound pressure level of a directional whistle shall be not more than 4 dB below the sound pressure level on the axis at any direction in the horizontal plane within ±45 degrees of the axis. The sound pressure level at any other direction in the horizontal plane shall be not more than 10 dB below the sound pressure level on the axis, so that the range in any direction will be at least half the range on the forward axis. The sound pressure level shall be measured in that one-third octave band which determines the audibility range.

(e) *Positioning of whistles.* When a directional whistle is to be used as the only whistle on a vessel, it shall be installed with its maximum intensity directed straight ahead.

A whistle shall be placed as high as practicable on a vessel, in order to reduce interception of the emitted sound by obstructions and also to minimize hearing damage risk to personnel. The sound pressure level of the vessel's own signal at listening posts shall not exceed 110 dB (A) and so far as practicable should not exceed 100 dB (A).

(f) *Fitting of more than one whistle.* If whistles are fitted at a distance apart of more than 100 metres, it shall be so arranged that they are not sounded simultaneously.

(g) *Combined whistle systems.* If due to the presence of obstructions the sound field of a single whistle or of one of the whistles referred to in paragraph 1(f) above is likely to have a zone of greatly reduced signal level, it is recommended that a combined whistle system be fitted so as to overcome this reduction. For the purposes of the rules a combined whistle system is to be regarded as a single whistle. The whistles of a combined system shall be located at a distance apart of not more than 100 metres and arranged to be sounded simultaneously. The frequency of any one whistle shall differ from those of the others by at least 10 Hz.

2. *Bell or Gong*

(a) *Intensity of signal.* A bell or gong, or other device having similar sound characteristics shall produce a sound pressure level of not less than 110 dB at 1 metre.

(b) *Construction.* Bells and gongs shall be made of corrosion-resistant material and designed to give a clear tone. The diameter of the mouth of the bell shall be not less than 300 mm for vessels of more than 20 metres in length, and shall be not less than 200 mm for vessels of 12 to 20 metres in length. Where practicable, a power-driven bell striker is recommended to ensure constant force but manual operation shall be possible. The mass of the striker shall be not less than 3 percent of the mass of the bell.

3. *Approval*

The construction of sound signal appliances, their performance and their installation on board the vessel shall be to the satisfaction of the appropriate authority of the State where the vessel is registered.

ANNEX IV

DISTRESS SIGNALS

1. The following signals, used or exhibited either together or separately, indicate distress and need of assistance:

(a) a gun or other explosive signal fired at intervals of about a minute;

(b) a continuous sounding with any fog-signalling apparatus;

(c) rockets or shells, throwing red stars fired one at a time at short intervals;

(d) a signal made by radiotelegraphy or by any other signalling method consisting of the group ... — — — ... (SOS) in the Morse Code;

(e) a signal sent by radiotelephony consisting of the spoken word "Mayday";

(f) the International Code Signal of distress indicated by N.C.;

(g) a signal consisting of a square flag having above or below it a ball or anything resembling a ball;

(h) flames on the vessel (as from a burning tar barrel, oil barrel, etc.)

(i) a rocket parachute flare or a hand flare showing a red light;

(j) a smoke signal giving off orange-coloured smoke;

(k) slowly and repeatedly raising and lowering arms outstretched to each side;

(l) the radiotelegraph alarm signal;

(m) the radiotelephone alarm signal;

(n) signals transmitted by emergency position-indicating radio beacons.

2. The use or exhibition of any of the foregoing signals except for the purpose of indicating distress and need of assistance and the use of other signals which may be confused with any of the above signals is prohibited.

3. Attention is drawn to the relevant sections of the International Code of Signals, the Merchant Ship Search and Rescue Manual and the following signals:

(a) a piece of orange-coloured canvas with either a black square and circle or other appropriate symbol (for identification from the air);

(b) a dye marker.

D Excerpts from Motorboat Act of 25 April 1940

AN ACT TO AMEND LAWS FOR PREVENTING COLLISIONS OF VESSELS, TO REGULATE THE EQUIPMENT OF CERTAIN MOTORBOATS ON THE NAVIGABLE WATERS OF THE UNITED STATES, AND FOR OTHER PURPOSES

Motorboat defined: inspection

Be it enacted by the Senate and House of Representatives of the United States of America in Congress assembled. That the word "motorboat" where used in this Act shall include every vessel propelled by machinery and not more than sixty-five feet in length except tugboats and towboats propelled by steam. The length shall be measured from end to end over the deck, excluding sheer: *Provided.* That the engine, boiler, or other operating machinery shall be subject to inspection by the Coast Guard, and to its approval of the design thereof, on all said motorboats, which are more than forty feet in length, and which are propelled by machinery driven by steam (46 U.S.C. 526.)

Classes of motorboats

SEC. 2. Motorboats subject to the provisions of this Act shall be divided into four classes as follows:

Class A. Less than sixteen feet in length.

Class 1. Sixteen feet or over and less than twenty-six feet in length.

Class 2. Twenty-six feet or over and less than forty feet in length.

Class 3. Forty feet or over and not more than sixty-five feet in length. (46 U.S.C. 526a.)

Lights

SEC. 3. Every motorboat in all weathers from sunset to sunrise shall carry and exhibit the following lights when under way, and during such time no other lights which may be mistaken for those prescribed shall be exhibited:

(a) Every motorboat of classes A and 1 shall carry the following lights:

First. A bright white light aft to show all around the horizon.

Second. A combined lantern in the fore part of the vessel and lower than the white light aft, showing green to starboard and red to port, so fixed as to throw the light from right ahead to two points abaft the beam on their respective sides.

(b) Every motorboat of classes 2 and 3 shall carry the following lights:

First. A bright white light in the fore part of the vessel as near the stem as practicable, so constructed as to show an unbroken light over an arc of the horizon of twenty points of the compass, so fixed as to throw the light ten points on each side of the vessel; namely, from right ahead to two points abaft the beam on either side.

Second. A bright white light aft to show all around the horizon and higher than the white light forward.

Third. On the starboard side a green light so constructed as to show an unbroken light over an arc of the horizon of ten points of the compass, so fixed as to throw the light from right ahead to two points abaft the beam on the starboard side. On the port side a red light so constructed as to show an unbroken light over an arc of the horizon of ten points of the compass, so fixed as to throw the light from right ahead to two points abaft the beam on the port side. The said side lights shall be fitted with inboard screens of sufficient height so set as to prevent these lights from being seen across the bow.

(c) Motorboats of classes A and 1 when propelled by sail alone shall carry the combined lantern, but not the white light aft, prescribed by this section. Motorboats of classes 2 and 3, when so propelled, shall carry the colored side lights, suitably screened, but not the white lights, prescribed by this section. Motorboats of all classes, when so propelled, shall carry, ready at hand, a lantern or flashlight showing a white light which shall be exhibited in sufficient time to avert collision.

(d) Every white light prescribed by this section shall be of such character as to be visible at a distance of at least two miles. Every colored light prescribed by this section shall be of such character as to be visible at a distance of at least one mile. The word "visible" in this Act, when applied to lights, shall mean visible on a dark night with clear atmosphere.

(e) When propelled by sail and machinery any motorboat shall carry the lights required by this section for a motorboat propelled by machinery only.

(f) Any motorboat may carry and exhibit the lights required by the Regulations for Preventing Collisions at Sea, 1960, Act of September 24, 1963 (77 Stat. 194-210; 33 U.S.C. 1051-1053, 1061-1094), as amended as lieu of the lights required by this section. (46 U.S.C. 526b.)

NOTE: On motorboats of classes A and 1 the aft white all around light or the 12 point white stern light may be located off the centerline.

Whistles

SEC. 4. Every motorboat of class 1, 2, or 3 shall be provided with an efficient whistle or other sound-producing mechanical appliance. (46 U.S.C. 526c.)

Bells

SEC. 5. Every motorboat of class 2 or 3 shall be provided with an efficient bell. (46 U.S.C. 526d.)

Exemptions for outboard racing motorboats

SEC. 9. The provisions of sections 4, 5, and 8 of

this Act shall not apply to motorboats propelled by outboard motors while competing in any race previously arranged and announced or, if such boats be designed and intended solely for racing, while engaged in such navigation as is incidental to the tuning up of the boats and engines for the race. (46 U.S.C. 526k.)

Pilot rules not required

SEC. 12. Motorboats shall not be required to carry on board copies of the pilot rules. (46 U.S.C. 526k.)

Authority to arrest for negligent operation

SEC. 15. Any officer of the United States authorized to enforce the navigation laws of the United States, shall have power and authority to swear out process and to arrest and take into custody, with or without process, any person who may commit any act or offense prohibited by section 13, or who may violate any provision of said section: *Provided*, That no person shall be arrested without process for any offense not committed in the presence of some one of the aforesaid officials: *Provided, further,* That whenever an arrest is made under the provisions of this Act, the person so arrested shall be brought forthwith before a commissioner, judge, or court of the United States for examination of the offense alleged against him, and such commissioner, judge, or court shall proceed in respect thereto as authorized by law in cases of crimes against the United States. (46 U.S.C. 526n.)

Penalty for other violations of Act

SEC. 16. If any motorboat or vessel subject to any of the provisions of this Act is operated or navigated in violation of this Act or any regulation issued thereunder, the owner or operator, either one or both of them, shall, in addition to any other penalty prescribed by law, be liable to a penalty of $100: *Provided*, That in the case of motorboats or vessels subject to the provisions of this Act carrying passengers for hire, a penalty of $200 shall be imposed on the owner or operator, either one or both of them, thereof for any violation of section 6, 7, or 8 of this Act or of any regulations pertaining thereto. For any penalty incurred under this section the motorboat or vessel shall be held liable and may be proceeded against by way of libel in the district court of any district in which said motorboat or vessel may be found. (46 U.S.C. 526o.)

Regulations; enforcement

SEC. 17. The Commandant of the Coast Guard shall establish all necessary regulations required to carry out in the most effective manner all of the provisions of this Act, and such regulations shall have the force of law. The Commandant of the Coast Guard or any officer of the Coast Guard authorized by the Commandant may, upon application therefor, remit or mitigate any fine, penalty, or forfeiture incurred under this Act or any regulation thereunder relating to motorboats or vessels, except the penalties provided for in section 14 hereunder. The Commandant of the Coast Guard shall establish such regulations as may be necessary to secure the enforcement of the provisions of this Act by any officer of the United States authorized to enforce the navigation laws of the United States. (46 U.S.C. 526p.)